World Wisdom
The Library of Perennial Philosophy

The Library of Perennial Philosophy is dedicated to the exposition of the timeless Truth underlying the diverse religions. This Truth, often referred to as the *Sophia Perennis*—or Perennial Wisdom—finds its expression in the revealed Scriptures as well as in the writings of the great sages and the artistic creations of the traditional worlds.

Introduction to Traditional Islam, Illustrated: Foundations, Art, and Spirituality appears as one of our selections in the Perennial Philosophy series.

Perennial Philosophy Series

In the beginning of the twentieth century, a school of thought arose which has focused on the enunciation and explanation of the Perennial Philosophy. Deeply rooted in the sense of the sacred, the writings of its leading exponents establish an indispensable foundation for understanding the timeless Truth and spiritual practices which live in the heart of all religions. Some of these titles are companion volumes to the Treasures of the World's Religions series, which allows a comparison of the writings of the great sages of the past with the perennialist authors of our time.

Introduction to Traditional Islam

Illustrated

Foundations, Art, and Spirituality

Jean-Louis Michon

Foreword by Roger Gaetani

World Wisdom

Selection of illustrations and book design by Susana Marín

Library of Congress Cataloging-in-Publication Data

Michon, Jean-Louis.
  Introduction to traditional Islam, illustrated : foundations, art, and spirituality / Jean-Louis
Michon ; foreword by Roger Gaetani.
      p. cm. — (Perennial philosophy series)
  Includes bibliographical references and index.
  ISBN 978-1-933316-51-2 (pbk. : alk. paper) 1. Islam—Essence, genius, nature. 2. Mysticism—
Islam. 3. Art, Islamic. 4. Civilization, Islamic. I. Title.
  BP163.M48 2008
  297—dc22
                                                              2008017097

Cover: Dome of the Harun-i Vilayat Mausoleum, Isfahan, Iran
Photograph by Susana Marín

Printed on acid-free paper in China.

For information address World Wisdom, Inc.
P.O. Box 2682, Bloomington, Indiana 47402-2682
www.worldwisdom.com

CONTENTS

Foreword   ix

Preface   xi

PART I

Islam: Foundations

1 Islam and Urban Civilization   4

   Urban Development in Islam's Earliest Period   4

   The Muslim Community   8

2 The Sources   10

   The Koran and the Proclamation of Divine Unity   10

   The Tradition of the Prophet   12

   Jurisprudence   13

3 The Pillars of Islam   16

   Prayer   17

   The Fast   25

   Alms-giving   26

   Pilgrimage   27

4 The Functions of the City   30

   Executive Power   32

   Judicial Authority   34

   Religious Instruction   35

   The Maintenance of Moral Standards and the Encouragement of

   Goodness   41

Epilogue   43

PART II

The Message of Islamic Art

1 Art: An Integral Part of Muslim Life   51

2 The Formal Languages   54

3 Art within the City, or How the Message of Divine Unity Becomes
   Imprinted in the Muslim Living Environment   59

     A Sanctuary with Multiple Cells   59

     The Religious Function: The Mosque   62

     The Other Functions of the City   63

     The Divine Mark of Calligraphy   66

     Infinite Radiation and Omnipresent Center   71

     God is Light   72

     Water as the Source of Life   77

     Representational Art is not Excluded   80

     Simple Life   82

     The God-loved Artisan   84

Epilogue   86

PART III

Music and Spirituality in Islam

1 A Controversial Question   91

2 The Philosopher-Musicologists   93

3 Sufis and the Spiritual Concert   96

4 The Elements of Musical Expression   99

     Instruments   99

     Melodic Modes   101

     Rhythm   102

     The Human Voice   103

5 Musical Genres   104

     The Call to Prayer   105

     Praises upon the Prophet   105

     Devotional Music of Shī'ite Iran   107

     The *Qawwālī* of India and Pakistan   108

     The Music of the Kurdish "People of the Truth"   109

     Spiritual Audition of Classical Music   110

Arabo-Andalusian Music 110

Iranian Music 113

Turkish Music 116

Hindustani Music 117

Popular Music 118

Epilogue 119

PART IV

The Way of the Sufis

1 The Mystical Quest in Islam: Scriptural and Historical Roots 123

2 The Way to God: Conjunction of Human Effort and Divine Effusion 126

Initiation 128

The Spiritual Master 129

Good Company 131

3 The Spiritual Meetings 133

Invocation 133

The *Wird* 136

The Hymns 137

The Sacred Dance 138

4 Spiritual Progress 143

"Know Thyself" 144

Perpetual Orison 145

The Three Stages of Certainty 147

Epilogue 148

List of Illustrations 150

Index 153

Biographical Notes 155

FOREWORD

To think that we can understand Islam through current headlines and the conflicting opinions of political pundits is sheer illusion. We might do better to review some bare facts: Islam is a monotheistic religion whose followers believe that it was revealed through the archangel Gabriel in stages to the Prophet Muhammad over the course of a number of years, starting in 610 AD and lasting until his death in 632. The holy book of Islam, the Koran, is a transcription in Arabic of these revelations. The Koran is the basis of Islamic law, belief, and practice, and is supplemented by the accounts of Muhammad's sayings and actions, and by the interpretations of religious scholars.

Our review of facts tells us that Islam rapidly expanded through conquest and trade, and that a highly developed civilization emerged which has remained a source of culture and pride to Muslims for well over a thousand years. To this day, over 1.5 billion Muslims (about a quarter of the world's population) share a strong sense of community and identity despite the fact that Islam—the majority religion in countries stretching from West Africa to Indonesia—spans many diverse peoples and lands. Most Muslims are not even Arabs, yet they all turn towards Mecca in prayer and recite the same holy words in Arabic. These bare facts are more helpful in understanding Islam than the acts and words of misguided fanatics; yet even more helpful would be a well qualified personal guide to introduce us to a multitude of ways through which we can approach the inner life of this faith.

It is difficult to imagine a time when the West has been more in need of a good personal guide to the world of Islam. But how will we know when we have found such a guide? With patience he will certainly explain to us the most important concepts that we must know in order to understand the Muslim way of life and thinking. His words will lead us to places where we can experience sights and sounds that broaden and deepen our understanding of that other civilization in a way that is just as powerful as any listing of facts and data. Along the way, our guide might introduce us to some notable people, or point out intriguing paths that lead to some remarkable places we might later explore more fully on our own, or he might pause to direct our attention to the chanting coming from a gathering of dervishes in a room high above the street. Of course, our guide must be fully aware of the gaps that exist between that other way of life and our own; he must tell us only the truth and leave out personal biases; and, finally, he must have the skill and geniality to communicate effectively. Readers of this book certainly have such a guide in Jean-Louis Michon.

It should be a comfort to readers, both Muslim and other, to learn that Dr. Michon's point of departure is that Islam is "an expression of the Universal Tradition". By this he means that there is and always has been a single source of Truth in the universe, and that this Truth has chosen to manifest Itself to various times and peoples in forms that are suited to those people. From this perspective, Islam, like other revealed traditions, is precious in and of itself because wherever one looks within its many aspects, the tradition bears the imprint of Providence. What we as outsiders must do is to learn how and where to look for this imprint. It may come as a surprise that such an attitude regarding the validity of other faiths is, in fact, deeply embedded in Islam itself. It is an article of faith for Muslims that there have been many prophets sent by God to many peoples and that these

1. *Opposite*: Tile work from the Alhambra, Granada, Spain

prophets must share the unflagging respect of believing Muslims. This results in a certain kinship between Muslims and other "People of the Book", primarily Jews and Christians. This, too, may be surprising to readers, but this book holds many such surprises. It is likely that some followers of other faiths who read these pages with open minds and hearts will, through their own familiarity with the sacred, come to comprehend something of the ancient kinship between Muslims and others who seek to know and to worship the One.

Besides the framework of the Universal Tradition mentioned above, Dr. Michon's approach in this book is notable in several other ways. First, he intertwines the spirit and development of the Islamic city with the other aspects of the religion. Here, the city is seen as a crystallization of the principles of the faith. From its arts, crafts, and architecture, to its government, to the clothing and assemblies of its citizens, the city demonstrates how a traditional society is steeped in constant reminders of the origin and the end of all bounty, virtue, and beauty—God. It is a reminder to us all of the possibilities of finding almost endless avenues of connecting spiritually to a higher reality, thus ennobling ourselves and paying due respect to the potential of those avenues. A ready example would be the traditional, and thus sacred, ambiance of a home. Dr. Michon makes the case that the role of the traditional city is to be a powerful force for individual and communal salvation. This is a challenging concept for modern people who often limit their religion to specific times and places outside their homes and everyday lives; yet to understand Traditional Islam we must understand that for Muslims it is natural for Islam, because of its sacredness and scope, to permeate all aspects of the individual and communal lives of believers.

This book is also notable in that it focuses a great deal of attention on art and music in Islam. Indeed, the well-chosen and often stunning illustrations that grace the pages of this book contribute greatly to its impact. Few writers have Jean-Louis Michon's degree of personal experience with Islamic art and music, and even fewer are able to penetrate beneath the forms to the spirituality within them. Although the discussions of art history or musical structures may at first seem peripheral to an introduction to the faith, patient reading will show that once again Dr. Michon uses these as a way to coax the spiritual essence of the forms to reveal themselves to us. The foreign words or ideas, though certainly useful to researchers, should not put off the general reader: One need not know the details of music theory to enjoy a symphony, but when we are alerted to the presence of patterns in a foreign work, new meanings can leap to our consciousness. The in-depth discussions of art and music establish for us one grand pattern, namely, that here, too, the Spirit enters the life of the individual and the community.

It is completely appropriate that the book should culminate in a section on Sufism, the personal quest for a "taste" of God's Presence. It is for this same goal, though with less exalted horizons, that all the other laws, practices, arts, and institutions of Islam primarily exist. Once again, we have a uniquely qualified guide in Dr. Michon. After his survey of Sufism, we are compelled to reflect that the source, namely Traditional Islam, which fed this kind of inwardness, peace, and virtue, could not be the same source that feeds the strident, militant version of the "religion" which claims the same name. For that realization, and much more, we owe our guide our heartfelt thanks.

ROGER GAETANI

PREFACE

More often than not a civilization will be pieced together starting from the material traces it has left. This is the way the archaeologists work when, their interest aroused by vestiges whose meaning remains partly obscure, they try to reconstitute the context in which objects that have been found assume their real importance. In the case of Islam, such traces abound, and many a traveler has been fascinated by them, from Marco Polo to Orientalist painters of the romantic and colonial periods, and modern tourists: auditive and visual traces, human encounters of a particular quality, ranging from the call to prayer of the muezzin heard at the first dawn spent in a Muslim land to the serene geometry of arabesques, and the warm and dignified welcome given by the artisan in his shop or the Bedouin in his tent.

It is not through such external signs, however, that I and others of my generation, who were students during the Second World War and had nothing but books by which to discover the world, became acquainted with Islam. We had to follow a very different course, starting from the inside, and it was through philosophers and mystics that Islam was revealed to us. From the outside, all what we had previously perceived about Islam had been forbidding, with a few strong images inherited from our "lay and compulsory" education: Roland at Roncevaux, Charles Martel at Poitiers, the Barbaresques, the conquest of Algeria and the "revolt" of Abdelkader, the only human impressions being those received during our provincial childhood, reduced to the chance encounters, all distances being carefully observed, with the "sidi" vendor of balloons and carpets.

In spite of what lay between us in the way of social and ideological prejudices, however, Islam brought an answer to our queries. This occurred at a crucial moment in contemporary history when, for many, the tragedy of the planetary conflict raised a new question about a number of acquired beliefs and values, such as the paternal ideals of social success, of the sovereign motherland—"State, what crimes have been committed in thy name!"—, and even those of a certain Christian moralism reduced to interdicts that had never been properly explained or justified. We felt an urge to find a raison d'être beyond these upheavals, to restructure a world that was on the verge of dislocation.

Already at that time, in the mid-forties, a few providentially gifted interpreters, such as René Guénon and other contributors to the journal *Études traditionnelles*, including Frithjof Schuon and Titus Burckhardt, had given the public access to the "lights of Islam" and other expressions of the Universal Tradition, the *Religio perennis* or, for Hindus, *sanātana dharma*, "The Eternal Law": through their writings, their clear expositions of Vedanta metaphysics and the existential monism of Islam, we acquired a certitude that there is a Supreme Principle, a non-manifest Absolute from which all manifestation, all

2. Sidi Halaoui minaret, Tlemcen, Morocco

creation derives without assuming a separate, independent existence. We also came to recognize degrees in this manifestation, each with its own rank and features. Once this need for causality had been satisfied, some of us felt eager to embark on what Lanza del Vasto had called in a contemporary narrative "The pilgrimage to the sources".

In 1946 I moved to Damascus where I stayed for three years, immersing myself in the Islamic culture as deeply as was compatible, without creating too much scandal, with my teaching position at the Lycée Franco-Arabe. I sought the company of students and teachers of religious science, took lessons in Koranic recitation and the Oriental lute, scoured the alleys of the old city and the slopes of Jabal Qāsiūn to visit sanctuaries and meet with saintly persons. Years later, I visited other parts of the Muslim world, from Morocco to India and the "Moros" communities of Mindanao, without ever feeling during these journeys that I was trespassing on foreign soil. It was as if the very first approach, based on ratiocination, had provided a key which, at the right moment, opened the doors of the "concrete" Islam with its faithful, its rites, its social etiquette, its art and craft productions; and as if no dichotomy had ever existed between the two paths that gave access to the world of Islam: the path of written teachings and the progression on the roads of the Orient.

It is the results of this double quest that I have attempted to assemble here, repeating by necessity a number of notions that are already familiar to readers conversant with Orientalist works, but hoping that these notions, cemented by a life's experience, will have acquired the backing of some persuasive evidence.

At a time when Islam often occupies the front pages of newspapers and when its image, bound up with political and other interests, is distorted, or even caricatured, by its detractors as well as by blinded zealots, I felt it might be worthwhile to evoke its original and lasting features, those which belong to a true civilization, construed to remind man of his mission as a caliph, or lieutenant of God on earth, and to help him fulfill this mission while actualizing the fulfillment of his noblest qualities.

JEAN-LOUIS MICHON

3. Carved calligraphy from the *mihrāb* of the Friday Mosque of Isfahan, Iran

PART I

ISLAM: FOUNDATIONS

PART I

ISLAM: FOUNDATIONS

In seventh century Arabia, a messenger was given a divine message. The message was the Koran, the revealed scripture of Islam, and from it flowed, like an immense system of tributaries, rivers, and seas, a body of laws and spiritual practices, a worldview and patterns of behavior that have imprinted countless generations of people from western Africa to Indonesia, a flowering of sciences and arts that became crowning achievements of vibrant civilizations, and, perhaps above all, from it there still flows an ever-present perfume that reminds each soul of that other world and dimension of existence that awaits after the joys and travails of this life are finished.

In addition to the Koran, the Islamic tradition has also been primarily shaped by the *Sunnah* of the Prophet Muhammad (the reports of his preferred personal practices) and the *Hadith* (his sayings). We can say that the religion of Islam gives life to a "tradition" not only because of its long history, but also because the touch of the sacred has extended to every significant aspect of the life of Muslims. This would include personal values of seeking knowledge, piety, peace, integrity, and so on. There are also community institutions such as the structures of courts, the collection of taxes, and even the calendar itself which reflect the influence of the religion. And then there are monuments of art and architecture, music, science, and literature, all of which are examples of Islamic principles taking on concrete forms. These overlapping dimensions of private and communal life, all touched by the sacred source of the Islamic revelation, together make up what is properly called "Traditional Islam".

It may be difficult for modern Westerners to appreciate or understand Traditional Islam, in some ways even more so today than previously. It is not the Islam that they see featured in current news headlines. It contrasts sharply with "militant", "fundamentalist", and "political" interpretations of Islam, all of which have turned against many aspects of traditional Islamic civilization mentioned above and throughout this book. This book highlights the enduring principles and foundations of the second largest religion in the world and shows how the Koran, *Sunnah*, Islamic art, culture, music, and spirituality, remain at the heart of this dynamic faith.

The characteristically monolithic nature of Islam, which is the religion of Divine Unity, strives to orientate the lives of individuals, as well as of societies, to the worship of the One God and to leave no domain, in the unfolding of human activities, exempt from the authority of Divine Law. This book illustrates the impact of religion on the urban society and on the very configuration of the city and the role of religious institutions.

4. Tile work detail from the Friday Mosque of Isfahan, Iran

5. *Opposite*: Entrance from the central courtyard to the prayer room of the Qarawiyyin Mosque, Fez, Morocco

In its broadest and primary sense, the Islamic city, like the city of antiquity—the *Civitas Romano,* for example—is none other than the great community of persons obeying its law. It then embraces all those who profess Islam, and coincides with the *ummah,* the "Nation" of which every Muslim recognizes and feels himself to be a citizen, whether he lives isolated or with a group, as a nomad or as a sedentary, as a townsman or as a countryman.

Some scholars have studied the Islamic urban way of life and asked "how the Muslims conceived virtuous life and built their habitat to realize it here on earth".[1] And, what gives Muslim civilization its unquestionable homogeneity? Traditional Islam provides the very foundation and cohesiveness of this homogeneity since the religious dimension tends to encompass and penetrate all aspects of life in the Islamic world. This religion whose dogmatic cornerstone and enduring theme is *tawḥīd,* the affirmation of Divine Unity, seeks to assert, above and through all the relativities of the here-below, the imprescriptible rights of the Lord of the Worlds.

1—ISLAM AND URBAN CIVILIZATION

❧ *Urban Development in Islam's Earliest Period*

Many indeed are the observers and historians of Islam who have remarked on an astonishing contrast within the geographical and human context where the Islamic Message first established itself: the Arabian Peninsula, inhabited mainly by nomadic Bedouins or semi-sedentaries, and the classical visage of the Muslim world as it was to emerge a bare few centuries later: a network of great cities from India

6. *Top left*: Jabal Nūr (Mount Hira), where Muhammad received his first revelation of the Koran from the Archangel Gabriel, Mecca, Saudi Arabia

7. *Above left*: The Mosque of ʿAlī in al-Khandaq, Medina, Saudi Arabia

8. *Right*: Jabal Ṭūr, the sacred mountain near Mecca, where Muhammad received numerous revelations

1. Cf. *The Islamic City*, R.B. Sergeant (ed.), selected papers from the colloquium held at the Middle East Center, Faculty of Oriental Studies, Cambridge, U.K., 19-23 July, 1976 (Paris: Unesco, 1980).

to the Far West between which there would flow and interflow, by land and sea, every kind of product as well as branches of knowledge, ideas, and cultures.

It is a fact that the propagation of Islam by the Arab armies and, even more, by the sheer conviction of the Message they carried with them, was accompanied by extraordinary urban development. This phenomenon took place in the three great areas to which the conquest first extended—namely: the Sassanid Empire in the North East (Mesopotamia and Iran), the Byzantine Empire (Syria and Egypt), and the previously Romanized West, now partly barbarized (North Africa and Spain). New towns appeared which were originally no more than fortified camps, such as Kufah and Basrah, founded in 157/637* during the Caliphate of 'Umar.** Their very first inhabitants, consisting of fighters in the Holy War, were supplemented by new converts and "protected persons" (Jews and Christians, all of them "People of the Book" subject to a head-tax but free as regards their persons, goods, and worship) at such a rapid pace that Kufah boasted a population of over 100,000 souls within thirty years, and Basrah over 200,000. The breakneck pace at which Baghdad, founded in 145/762 by the Caliph al-Mansur, was built by 100,000 workers, who were also its first inhabitants, meant that the Abbasid capital was the home—forty years later—of some 2,000,000 citizens and was the greatest metropolis of its age. Many more examples could be adduced: the creation of Fustāt—the future Cairo—by Amr in 19/641, of Kairouan by 'Uqbah

9. *Above*: The oratory of Salman Farsi in al-Khandaq, Medina, Saudi Arabia

10. *Below*: The oasis of Medina, Saudi Arabia

Publisher's Notes:

* Islam has its own calendar. The first year begins in 622 A.D. with the Hegira, when the Prophet and the first Muslims took flight from Mecca to Medina. Throughout this book, the dates used are given as Islamic/Christian. This means the first is the Hegira date followed by the Gregorian date. We have deleted the H. and the A.D. for reasons of space.

** In early Islam, the Caliph was the "head of state" or spiritual leader and temporal ruler of the Muslim Community. The Caliphate was the Islamic form of government.

11. The city of Medina, view from the south-east side; the dome built by the Ottomans in the 17th century covers the tomb of the Prophet Muhammad and his two close Companions, Abū Bakr and 'Umar

12. Side arcade of the Great Mosque of Kairouan, Tunisia

13. Courtyard *qibla* side of the Great Mosque of Kairouan, Tunisia

in 48/670, and of Tunis several years later, followed by Almería (756) and Fez (807). There were, moreover, ancient cities everywhere which, having fallen into decadence, found renewed vigor and prosperity with their entry into the *Pax Islamica* such as Damascus, Balkh, Bukhara and Samarkand, or Córdoba and Seville.

How are we to account for a town planning vocation as precocious and strongly affirmed as this in the world of Islam? City organization was doubtless not unknown to the Arab conquerors; Mecca, where Muhammad was born in the year 570 and where his prophetic vocation was proclaimed, had long been an urban grouping of real importance as a nexus of the caravan trade in the Arabian peninsula and a center of pilgrimage sheltering the statues of numerous divinities in the Temple of the Ka'bah. But above all, there has been the experience of Medina, the "City of the Prophet" where Muhammad had found asylum at the time of the Hegira or "emigration" from Mecca—calculated as the first year of the Islamic calendar—in the year 622 of the Christian era and where the bases of the Muslim community and its organization were forged.

It was at Medina during the ten years' residence there of the Prophet, until his death, together with his companions—like himself emigrees from Mecca or "Helpers" from Medina—that the Muslim community was endowed with its basic institutions. Medina was—and to a large extent has never ceased to be—the model Islamic city, whose example inspired the founders of the first cities already referred to, just as it has never ceased to serve as a point of reference down the centuries for the reflections and modes of action of Muslim lawmakers and rulers. Without the firm imprint inherited from this first city of Islam under the three-fold influence of the revealed Message, the personality of Muhammad, and the communal discipline acquired by the first believers, it is inconceivable that the fighters of the Holy War would have been able—even supposing them to have been capable of their lightning conquest—to implant their unmistakably Islamic ideals and lifestyle in lands so widespread and variegated, certain of which were themselves heirs to very ancient cultures.

14. The Amr Mosque, Cairo, Egypt

15. The Great Mosque of Córdoba, Spain

16. Courtyard of the Mosque of Ibn Tulun, Cairo, Egypt

True, the Conquest did not entail the destruction of ancient cities or of their structure. It remained essentially a matter of fighters and organized armies, and it encountered no great resistance on the part of populaces chafing under the yoke of the Byzantines or Sassanids. Its very speed was favorable to a kind of evolution which, however profound, did not overthrow the old order but facilitated its reshaping and adaptation into new frameworks of sufficient strength and breadth to be able to impose their standards without, however, effacing particular regional and local characteristics.[2]

17. Iraqi miniature depicting the city of Medina with the tombs of the Prophet, Abū Bakr, and ‘Umar, 16th century

❧ *The Muslim Community*

The success achieved by Islam in building up urban communities is not unconnected with the insistence the Koran places on the evocation of historical or allegorical events which are relevant to human groups—namely: nations and cities to which Divine messengers were sent, and no people has been denied Revelation.

However, the greater part of these nations and cities displayed ingratitude and sinfulness for which they incurred the Divine wrath: "And how many cities have We destroyed!" (Koran 7: 4).* "God coineth the parable of a city; it stood in safety and at peace; there flowed to it riches in abundance from every side; then it denied the blessings of God. God then made its people taste the tenors of hunger and fear in punishment for their deeds" (16: 112). "When We desire to destroy a city, We intimate consent to them that live in luxury and they abandon themselves to iniquity. Then is the word realized against it and We destroy it utterly" (17: 16).

In order to avoid the repetition of these evils, the Islamic community is bound to be virtuous and faithful to its commitments: "Ye are the best community raised up for men; ye commend what is reasonable; ye forbid what is blameworthy; ye believe in God" (3: 110). It received the gift of the "just mean" (2: 143). It forms an organic whole in which each element is at home: "Believer is to believer as the mutually upholding sections of a building", declared the Prophet in a much-quoted *hadīth*.** And he also said: "Ye will see the Muslims in their goodness, affection, and fellow-feeling form as it were a single body which, when one member is ailing, seeks to share out its sleeplessness and fever throughout that body." Finally, he gave an assurance that: "My community shall never be unanimous in error"—a declaration which was to have considerable repercussions in introducing the principle of *ijmā‘*, the consensus of believers, as a source for the elaboration of law. This solidarity is translated in Muslim law into the existence of a collective statute of obligation called the "duty of sufficiency" which exempts an individual believer from a compulsory legal duty from the moment that a sufficient number of the faithful join together to carry it out. This applies, for example, to the prayer for the dead, the Holy War (*jihād*), and the fulfillment of tasks requiring a thorough acquaintance with religious knowledge.

2. On urban development in the first centuries of Islam, cf. M. Lombard, "L'évolution urbaine pendant le Haut Moyen Âge", *Annales E.S.C.* (1957), 7-28 and, by the same author, *L'Islam dans sa Première Grandeur* (VIIIe-XIes) (Paris, 1971), chap. VI.

Publisher's Notes:

*Throughout this book, any references in parentheses whose sources are not specifically identified are from the Koran. The first number in these references is the *sūrah*, or chapter, and the second the *ayat*, or verses, cited from that chapter.

** The word *hadīth* is often translated as "tradition", meaning a report of the deeds and sayings of the Prophet Muhammad.

Certainly, in his conduct, a man commits himself alone and it is he alone who will appear before the Supreme Judge to answer for his actions. However, the bond which links him to the social body is so tight that he depends for his salvation largely upon those around him and upon the more-or-less favorable circumstances that prevail there for the accomplishment of revealed Law. "Verily, man is in loss, save only them that believe and perform good works, and exhort one another to Truth and exhort one another to patience" (103: 2-3), says the Koran, stressing in the latter part of the verse the importance of mutual admonition in the fundamental virtues.

This enduring combination of effort deployed by each man to submit to the will of the Divine Legislator, and of the communal framework which serves as a support and aid to this effort, is the most outstanding characteristic of the Islamic city. It will emerge again at each stage of our study in analyzing various "individual obligations" whose collective implications and constituent elements we shall not be able to overlook; in the Muslim city, the striving after individual salvation involves *ipso facto* the sacralization of the social, whilst inversely the community entrusted with the Divine Message, wise institutions, and the example of the just conserves their content for the benefit of its members.

18. Page from a pilgrimage guide depicting the Ka'bah in Mecca, 1582

The governance of God, the One and Only Lord and Absolute Monarch, and the equality of men in the sight of God, identically dependent upon and subject to Divine Law, each being nonetheless

19. Pilgrims around the Ka'bah in Mecca, Saudi Arabia

responsible for his actions and taking upon himself the obligations which devolve from this law—these two characteristics summarize the structure of the Muslim community which has rightly been described as an "egalitarian theocracy" and also as a "normocracy", this last notion laying stress on the natural constraint exercised by the Divine Law.[3]

2—THE SOURCES

The institutions of Islam are founded upon three sources: the Koran, the Tradition of the Prophet (*Sunnah*), and the written and oral teachings of jurists. It is the jurists who gave Muslim law its various "schools" but it is the two first sources—the Koran and the *Sunnah*—to which no scholar can fail to refer, which give it its identity and cohesion.

❧ *The Koran and the Proclamation of Divine Unity*

The Book of God "sent down" upon the Prophet Muhammad and "recited" by him to the community of mankind contains in its 114 chapters all the essential elements of Islamic "dogma" and law (*sharī'ah*). Its essential message is the proclamation of Divine Unity (*al-tawḥīd*), the absolute Transcendence of the Principle in regard to all manifestation and the status of total dependence on the part of the creature to the Supreme Craftsman. This message is condensed into the two formulae of the "attestation of faith" (*shahādah*), the utterance of which confers on every man of right intent the status of a Muslim. The first formula declares that "There is no god other than the One and Only God"; the second that "Muhammad is the messenger of God".

The first formula with its twofold movement of negation and affirmation expresses on the one hand the unreality of everything that does not contain its sufficient cause in itself, namely: the created world and what it holds, and on the other hand, the sole reality of the Absolute Being. The evidential strength of this imposes itself upon the understanding and compels adherence, in the first instance, of an intellectual order.

The second formula has a more personalized and voluntarist content. It implies not only the acceptance of Muhammad's prophetic mission, but also adherence to everything contained in the revealed Message. It also involves the acceptance of Muhammad as a guide and model for mankind and, consequently, the wish to conform to the practice (*Sunnah*) initiated by the Prophet.

Thus, a Muslim who bears witness to the divine Unity is not simply making a profession of monotheism; he is, at the same time, committing himself to obeying the law prescribed by the Koran and exemplified by the *Sunnah*. And this commitment becomes a kind of renewal of the pact of submission entered into with God the Omnipotent by souls at the instant of their creation: "Am I not your Lord?" "Indeed!" they agreed (7: 172). Thus, to utter the attestation of faith assumes the

20. Carved inscription of the name of Muhammad, Mausoleum of Sultan Oljaitu, Soltaniyah, Iran

3. On these concepts, see: L. Gardet, *La Cité musulmane* (Paris, 1961), chap. II and S.H. Nasr, *Traditional Islam in the Modern World* (New York: Routledge, Chapman & Hall, 1987). In the second work, the author makes a critical analysis of the so-called "fundamentalist" movements and their argumentations, demonstrating their anti-traditional character and their borrowings from a purely profane mentality.

meaning of a "remembrance" (*dhikr*) of the Primordial Covenant and this is true of all actions, no less than of all thoughts, by which a sincere Muslim will tend to draw close to God and to actualize in his own human and limited substance a unity of behavior and intent which will be a reflection of Divine Unity in his earthly life.

Proclamation of Oneness and remembrance of God—such are the essential goals to which the Koran unremittingly urges believers, and the means it indicates for realizing these goals are manifold, appealing to all the faculties with which man is endowed, aiming at weaving the sacred into his temporal dimension no less than the space in which he evolves, and into his innermost being no less than his family and social surroundings. Thus it is that he is enjoined, apart from the strictly obligatory practices of his religion—about which we shall speak later—to read the Divine Book (73: 4; 17: 78) and to invoke the Name of God, (in Arabic, *Allāh*) (87: 1, 15), and His "most beautiful Names" (17: 110), and also to utter certain formulae which celebrate and praise the Almighty, thank Him for His blessings, implore His help and protection, and remind us that He is the Unique Cause, the beginning and end of all things. All these forms of *dhikr* impose themselves upon him to punctuate a great number of the actions of his everyday life. The practice of worship, no less than the injunctions which regulate

21. Calligraphies of the Divine Name, *Allāh* (God), and the name of Muhammad; from a Turkish collection of Koran *sūrah*s

22. Pages from an Egyptian Koran; Rayhani script with *sūrah* headings in ornamental Eastern Kufic, 14th century

social life, even those which govern infringements of rules instituted by revealed Law have, in the last analysis, no higher function than to keep and guide believers into the "straight path" whereto are led, according to the words of the *Fātihah*, the opening chapter of the Koran (see fig. 154), "those that God hath blessed".

Beyond actions, the Koran exalts the virtues, which are like reflections in the human soul of the Divine Qualities. Submission to God (*islām*) which is what makes a man a Muslim, leads back to Him who is Peace (*al-Salām*) just as patience (*sabr*) is to pause whenever God, who is the Patient (*al-Sabūr*) *par excellence*, decrees pause. By following the injunction to be equitable, since "equitability is close to piety" (5: 8) believers—particularly those entrusted with positions of authority or council within the collectivity—will be true servants of God, who calls Himself "the Just" (*al-'Adl*).

These few indications should suffice to show how *tawhīd*, the proclamation of Divine Unity, which is the *raison d'être* of the Koranic Message, works to model the life and innermost substance of each member of the Muslim community and to enter in concrete fashion into city institutions.

✥ *The Tradition of the Prophet* (Sunnah)

The Prophet Muhammad is in some way the Koran in act. He is the intermediary providentially chosen not only to transmit to men the contents of the revealed Book but also to direct them on the path of return towards the One and Only God. He is at the same time the bearer of a particular message, Islamic law, and a shining manifestation of Universal Truth (*al-Haqq*). It is these two aspects that are referred to in the designations "Prophet" (*Nabī*) and "Envoy" (*Rasūl*).

The Koran enjoins believers to "obey God and His Envoy" (8: 1). Even more, it gives them the Prophet as "a fine example for whomsoever hopeth on God and the Last Day and remembereth God much" (33: 21). Hence the importance accorded by the first Companions, by those who followed them and, later, by the Muslim community as a whole, to collecting the sayings and counsels of the Prophet, and even his acts and gestures, to pondering them and putting them into practice.

This practice of the Prophet was brought together in the third century of the Hegira, in the great collections of sayings called *hadith*, which the traditionalists—Bukhārī, Muslim, Ibn Māja, Abū Dāwūd, Tirmīdhī, Nasā'ī—compiled with a degree of care no less than that which had moved the first Caliphs: Abū Bakr, 'Umar, and 'Uthmān, to establish a complete and definitive recension of the text of the Koran.

The *hadīth* provides an abundance of historical, formal, and practical detail on the beliefs, no less than on the acts of worship, laid down in the Koran. It contains invaluable information on the circumstances of Revelation, as well as spiritual and moral directives applicable to the various circumstances of individual and social life.

Occasionally, it even records aspects of Muhammad's behavior

23-24. Pages from a Maghrebi collection of *hadith*, Morocco, 1204

which, when assumed by the community, raised certain ancient Arab customs to the ranks of a religious tradition. Thus sanctioned and carried to the furthest confines of the Muslim world, these practices were to contribute to no mean extent to endowing the Muslim city and its inhabitants with certain of their characteristics. Such, for example, are the conventions governing the reception of guests, preparing and eating food, hygiene and care of the person (the use of henna and certain perfumes, the way of cutting the hair and beard), etc.

25. The Mosque of the Prophet in Medina, Saudi Arabia; view of *al-Rawdah*, the area next to the tomb of the Prophet

❧ *Jurisprudence*

Neither the Koran nor the *Sunnah* present themselves as coherent and organized collections of religious Law. Their prescriptions are spare, sometimes hardly elaborated. Moreover, these two sources are often silent on points of law which arise in proportion as the geographical extension of the *dār al-Islām*, and the tremendous cultural, social, and economic changes resulting therefrom, cause new needs to be felt.

During the thirty years after the death of Muhammad (632-661) the four "rightly guided" Caliphs: Abū Bakr, 'Umar, 'Uthman, and 'Alī, as well as their lieutenants, posted to the provinces of the new empire—all of them former Companions of the Prophet well versed in religious knowledge—governed the community according to the laws of the Koran. During this period, which Muslim sentiment still views, together with the ten Medina years, as Islam's "golden age", spiritual authority and temporal power continued to be united, as

26. The two formulae of the "attestation of faith" (*shahādah*); Turkish tile, 16th century

in Muhammad's lifetime, in the person of the Caliph. The only law recognized as such was the *sharī'ah* even when it made allowances, in the interests of handling current affairs, for customs and practices already well-established in the conquered lands.

However, with the Umayyad Dynasty, there gradually emerged a disassociation between the political and administrative power of the Caliph, who was concerned above all to establish and consolidate his temporal power, and authority in religious affairs which was handed over to judges entrusted with applying the *sharī'ah*. It was at this point that scholars of the law, moved by the desire to restore to Islam its original purity and homogeneity, occupied themselves with collecting all the prescriptions necessary for the conduct of the Islamic community into coherent compilations of doctrine. Basing themselves upon the Koran and the *Sunnah*, they filled out what they found therein by an effort of research (*ijtihād*) which, in order to resolve matters not explicitly covered by the two great traditional sources (the Koran and the *Sunnah*) depended either upon personal opinion (*rāy*), analogy (*qiyās*) or—again—upon the unanimous consensus (*ijmā'*) of the community of believers as expressed by its doctors of religious science.

This endeavor to codify jurisprudence resulted in the emergence of the four "methods" (*madhhab*, a word often translated as "rite" or "school") of Sunnite Islam.[4] In all cases, it deals with the whole body of prescriptions governing the actions of believers down to small details; actions which are obligatory, recommended, permitted, blameworthy, or forbidden, whether it be a question of acts of worship, social behavior, or penalties which have to be applied to infringements of legal prescriptions.

Very roughly, the schools and their respective areas of predominant authority are as follows:

a) the Malikite school of Malik ibn Anas (died 795) covers at the present moment North and Central Africa, Upper Egypt, the Sudan, and West Africa;

b) the Hanifite school of Abū Hanifah (died 767) which was adopted by the Ottomans, is today the most extensive and is found in Turkey, Syria, India, Southeast Asia and also in China;

c) the Shafi'ite school of Imām Shāfi'ī (died 820) covers Egypt, the Hijaz, Southern Arabia, East and Meridional Africa and shares Southeast Asia with the Hanifite rite;

d) the Hanbalite school, founded by Ahmad ibn Hanbal (died 855) is today limited to Arabia (Nejd).

From the religious viewpoint, the four schools are considered to be equally valid and it is perfectly acceptable for a Muslim to choose his own school and even to change it during his lifetime, particularly if he should change his place of residence and wish to conform to the rite of a new community.

The differences between the orthodox schools are, in the first place, methodological and are based on the particular method each founder used in variously elaborating the rulings of law; analogy

27. The Scribe; detail from the frontispiece of *The Epistles of the Sincere Brethren* (Ikhwān al-Safā'), Baghdad, Iraq, 1287

4. A resume of this is to be found in: *Encyclopedia of Islam*, new edition (E.I.), article: *FIKH*.

(*qiyās*) is accepted by all of them, but opinion (*rāy*) is distrusted by Shāfi'ī; *ijmā'* (*consensus doctorum*) was interpreted by Shāfi'ī as the unanimous agreement of scholars at a particular period, but was limited by Malik to the scholars of Medina and by Ibn Hanbal to the Prophet's Companions. These conceptions bring about certain variants with practical consequences that are sometimes of importance for the modalities of legal rulings, whether these be interpreted according to the letter (Malikism, Hanbalism) or in the spirit of the law (Shafi'ism, Hanafism) and according to the degree in which elements of local customary law (Medinese, Roman/Byzantine, Sassanid, Talmudic, or Christian from the Eastern churches) are given a place insofar as these are compatible with the religious concepts of Islam; on this last point, for example, the Hanbalite school would prove to be particularly strict and refractory as regards the introduction of usages considered to be reprehensible "innovations" (*bid'ah*).

Established at the beginning of the Abbassid Caliphate in the 3rd/9th century, the schools of jurisprudence have survived down to the present day and have never ceased to feed the speculations and arguments of the doctors of the law. Meanwhile, they have hardly evolved in any way and, with certain exceptions, such as the notable case of the Salafiyyah who hark back to the authority of Ibn Taymiyyah, the celebrated Hanbalite of the 8th/14th century, they have sought to revise neither the principles nor indeed the application of the law in order to adapt them to new social or economic needs. Drawing their substance from the state of affairs prevailing in the Prophet's day and under the first four caliphs, they constitute a kind of ideal law which it would seem impious and dangerous to try and bend to changing conditions.

Rather different, however, is the picture presented by jurisprudence as constituted in the so-called Shī'ite "faction" (*Shī'ah*) of the Muslim community. For Shī'ites, "partisans of 'Alī", it is 'Alī himself who, as the son-in-law and cousin of the Prophet, should legitimately have succeeded Muhammad as leader and guide of the Muslim community. The actions of the first three "rightly guided Caliphs" as recognized by the Sunnites are not, for the Shī'ites, a source of law. On the contrary, 'Alī and his imām descendants—twelve for the Duodecimans, seven for the Ismā'īlīs, and five for the Zaidīs—are the inheritors of the "light of Muhammad" and thereby the predestined interpreters of the external religious Law and expounders of the inner meaning of Revelation.

Limiting our attention to Twelve Imām Shī'ism which, as the official religion of Iran, is the most widespread, claiming half the population of Iraq and important groups of faithful in India, Pakistan, Afghanistan, and the Lebanon, we find that it grounds its law in the Koran and the Tradition of the Prophet (*hadīth*), as do the Sunnites and then on the teaching of 'Alī and the other imāms, in particular the fourth (Zayn al 'Ābidīn), the fifth (Muhammad al-Bāqir), the sixth (Ja'far as-Sādiq), and the eighth ('Alī al-Ridā) who were eminent theologians. The twelfth imām, Muhammad al-Mahdī, plays a special role in the

28. Abu Zaïd delivering a sermon at the Barga'id Mosque; from the *Maqāmāt of al-Harīrī*, Baghdad, Iraq, 1230

formation of Shī'ite law, or rather, in its extension to new situations; despite his occultation in the year 329/940, the "Master of Time" still dwells among men and gives spiritual guidance to men qualified to apply personal reflection (*ijtihād*) to problems of jurisprudence.

Thus, institutionally speaking, there appear to be two main traits which typify Twelve Imām Shī'ism in relation to all the Sunnite schools: on the one hand, the Shī'ite conception of the head of the Muslim community as not only a political leader and the guardian of the law but also as the holder of an initiatory and esoteric function—and, on the other hand, the continuing role played by *ijtihād*, with inspiration derived from the imam, in the evolution of law or the development of theology. Historically speaking, Twelve Imām Shī'ites no longer expect that any political and spiritual authority answering to every criterion of legitimacy will be able to take the destiny of the Muslim community in hand until the reappearance of the last imam. On this point their perspective is, as it were, trans-historical and dependent upon their expectation of the Mahdī. Sunnite Islam, on the contrary, will never cease to work for the restoration of the Caliphate, at both the practical and theoretical level, by elaborating rules of government sufficient at least to safeguard the appearance of the institution. At the level of the elaboration of jurisprudence, the respective positions of Sunnism and Shī'ism are, one might say, reversed; in Sunnite circles, it is generally felt that "the gates of *ijtihād* are closed" ever since the building up of the four great juridical systems which first of all formulated the principles of law and then, in the space of a few generations, drew detailed applications from them. Only juridical recommendations (*fatwā*) may be made bearing on specific points and based on precedent, whereas in Twelve Imām Shī'ism, *ijtihād* is still practiced and is able to formulate authoritative rulings to extend religious law to new conditions.[5]

These divergent positions nevertheless reveal an identical preoccupation—namely: to keep the community of believers within the order instituted by revealed Law. Therefore, beyond differences of interpretation—which Muslim wisdom sees as deriving from the Divine Goodness as expressed by the saying *ikhtilāf al-'ulamā' rahmah* ("the disagreements of the learned are a mercy")—Shī'ite and Sunnite Islam, as well as their various branches or schools, both make the same imprint, identical in time and space, on the followers of Islam and on their cities.

29. Tile work in Kufic script with the name 'Alī, Darb-e Imam Mausoleum, Isfahan, Iran

30. Inscribed brick in Kufic script with the names *Allāh*, 'Alī, and Muhammad, Turkey

5. Cf. S.H. Nasr, *Ideals and Realities of Islam* (London: Allen and Unwin, 1966), chap. VI, where the points of divergence and convergence between Sunnite and Shī'ite Islam (including Isma'ilism) are very lucidly outlined.

3—THE PILLARS OF ISLAM

Among the institutions common to all Muslims, there are four which, together with the twofold attestation of faith already discussed (*shahādah*), form the five "pillars of worship" namely: prayer, fasting, alms, and pilgrimage. These four principal devotions have often been likened to the four angles forming the base of a pyramid of which the *shahādah*, the proclamation of *tawhīd*, is the summit. This likeness illustrates very adequately the position of the individual believer whose existence is, as it were, placed in the space marked out by the sloping walls of the pyramid and led thereby to the apex, symbolizing the divine Unity. The same figure could also serve to represent the entire Muslim community which, additionally, is contained within the framework of the *shariʿah* and is pointed thereby at Heaven. The religious life of a Muslim shows a particularly insistent superimposition of both pictures, which involves no confusion, but works to add a collective dimension and meaning to the ritual acts performed by an individual, either implicitly as in solitary prayers and fasting or explicitly as in the communal prayers, alms, and pilgrimage.

❧ *Prayer*

The prayer is the kernel of Islam, the rite whose sanctifying power contributes most richly to each brick in the communal edifice and to its cohesion. The unifying force of the Koran, which is in Arabic, pervades many aspects of the individual Muslim's life. Thus, Arabic, the sacred language of Islam, provides unity to the Muslim community whether the Muslims live in Arab countries, Pakistan, Europe, or the United

31. The double *shahādah*, the two formulae of the "attestation of faith"

32. Prayer hall and *miḥrāb* of the Great Mosque of Kairouan, Tunisia

33. Planispheric astrolabe used to
determine the time of the prayers,
Iran, 12th century

34. Compass to determine the
direction to Mecca (*qiblah*), Iran,
19th century

35. *Top right*: *Miḥrāb* and *minbar* of
the Sultan Hassan Mosque, Cairo,
Egypt

36. *Bottom right*: Prayer hall of the
Suleymaniye Mosque, Istanbul,
Turkey

States of America. The Islamic prayers (*salāt*), are recited in Arabic no matter from which country the Muslim originates. Muslims pray five times a day facing the Ka'bah in Mecca. The direction of the Ka'bah in Mecca is indicated by the *mihrāb* in the mosque (see figs. 32, 35, 38, 132, 134 & 155). Here is not the place to analyze the formulae, mostly Koranic, and gestures which make the prayer into a complete invocation involving the sacralization of the body and the concentration of the soul, but we cannot pass over in silence the role played in the ordering of the ritual by the two conditions of earthly existence—time and space.

The prayer said five times daily: at dawn, midday, mid-afternoon, sunset, and after nightfall, punctuates with its rhythm the entire life of the individual from puberty to death; by its continuous renewal, it stamps upon time's passing the mark of that unique instant when the primordial Pact to adore their Lord was first joined by souls.

In the spatial context there is a like reduction to unity; the prayer starts in an upright stance, the vertical position proper to man, "God's vicegerent on earth" (Koran 2: 30 and *passim*), endowed from the moment of his creation "with the fairest rectitude" (95: 4). Each of the faithful is thus made to stand erect, as a pontiff, and positioned like an axis towards which God sends down His Favor and spreads it upon the earth. The horizontal orientation of the *qiblah* pointing towards Mecca brings about a symbolic regrouping of all believers at the spot where

37. *Left*: Pilgrims praying in front of the Ka'bah, Mecca, Saudi Arabia

38. Praying in the Great Mosque of Kairouan, Tunisia

39. Praying in the Mosque of Paris, France

40. Praying in the Friday Mosque of Isfahan, Iran

Abraham built a temple to the One God, which is the tangible trace on earth of the *axis mundi*.

Prayer, like fasting, is obligatory upon every "responsible" Muslim, that is every adult of sound mind. Performed communally, it is said to be "twenty-seven times better than that performed in solitude" (*hadīth*) doubtless because it brings together in the ranks of the faithful both rich and poor, weak and powerful, without distinction and thus actualizes in concrete fashion the ideal of the perfect city whose inhabitants, like the Angels in the celestial spheres, celebrate the Creator's glory in unison.

Certain conditions which precede or accompany the performance of prayer have considerably influenced the design and functioning of the cities of Islam. They are: the state of ritual purity, by means of the

41. Praying in the courtyard of the mud-brick Friday Mosque at Ibb, Yemen

42. Praying in nature, Sudan

43. Praying in the Friday Mosque of Delhi, India

44. Praying in nature, Afghanistan

45. A guardian praying in the courtyard of the Madrasa Ben 'Ananiya, Fez, Morocco

greater or lesser ablution; respect for the time of prayer; the facing towards Mecca; the existence of a site large enough to accommodate all the faithful at the communal prayers on Friday at midday which are obligatory in all important centers of population.

The first requirement led to the provision of lavatories, pools, fountains, and public baths, the domes of which are sufficient to acclaim the presence of a Muslim city. The second gave birth to the functions of the *muwaqqit*, an official who works out timetables, and the muezzin who delivers the call to prayer; it led to the construction of minarets and, in certain capital cities, of astronomical observatories. The last two requirements determined how mosques were to be built and their liturgical requirements met: a prayer-hall extended in breadth, with a

46. Ablution fountain of al-Muayyad Mosque, Cairo, Egypt; 47. Ablution fountain, Morocco

48. Performing the ritual ablution before prayers, Pakistan

49. Ablution fountain of the Wazi Khan Mosque, Lahore, Pakistan

50. Ablution fountain of the Qarawiyyin Mosque, Fez, Morocco

51. Cupola of the Tairuzi public bath (*ḥammām*) in Damascus, Syria; **52**. Fountain of al-'Attarin, Fez, Morocco;
53. Ablution fountain of the Mahabat Khan Mosque, Pakistan

54. Prayer hall of the Qarawiyyin Mosque, Fez, Morocco; **55**. *Mihrāb* and *minbar* of the Aqsunghur Mosque, Cairo, Egypt

56. Shah Mosque, Lahore, Pakistan; **57**. Jame (Friday) Mosque, Isfahan, Iran

niche (*miḥrāb*) to indicate the *qiblah* and a pulpit (*minbar*) where the *imām* delivers his exhortation before the Friday prayers.

The mosque is not exclusively a place of prayer but also a meeting point or forum where the city's news is exchanged. It is a center of religious education where children and adults of all conditions sit in a circle, frequently after nightfall, to chant the Koran or to listen to the teaching of a scholar (*faqīh*); often it is a refuge where beggars, vagabonds, and the oppressed can find shelter and asylum and receive the alms or food generously dispensed by the community at places of worship.

The communal prayer is at times performed outside the center of the mosque, as is the case when the two great feasts are celebrated by Muslims to mark the end of the Pilgrimage and the Fast of Ramadan. The faithful then make their way in a crowd, to the *masalla*, situated outside the walls of the mosque, frequently close to the cemeteries, to pray in the open air facing a wall which shows the *qiblah*. These acts of grace in which the whole community participates—when thousands of foreheads are pressed to the ground and raised in a uniform movement in a silence broken only by the great cry of the *takbīr*—the formula *Allāhu akbar* ("God is most Great!")—are among the most eloquent manifestations of the reality and vitality of the Islamic city.

✦ *The Fast*

One needs to have lived in a Muslim town during the month of Ramadan to understand how much a rite performed individually gains in strength—if not in depth—by being practiced simultaneously by an entire people. Even before the sacred month starts, during which the fast must be observed from dawn till sunset, the city trembles with joyful anticipation. For, despite the very real trials of hunger and even more, of thirst during the hot afternoons, the whole month flows by in an atmosphere of joy. In many of the fasters one is aware of a feeling of release, as of one who is discharging a just debt and of pride at being able to sacrifice habits and to forego the satisfaction of pressing appetites. Heroic emulation grips everyone, even very young children who seethe with the desire to do as their elders are doing. Although Koranic law expressly exempts the sick, travelers, women approaching child-birth, and very old people from fasting, they nonetheless practice it assiduously. Many Muslims who do not practice their religion during the rest of the year, fast and pray during the sacred month and none would risk breaking the fast, except in secret.

58. Al-Bourdeni Mosque, Cairo, Egypt

59. Koranic teaching at the al-Azhar Mosque, Cairo, Egypt

The mosques are never empty at night. Circles are formed around readers of the Koran and preachers. Lengthy supererogatory prayers are recited communally or in solitude and special rogations are said for the absent, travelers, the sick, and prisoners. The twenty-seventh night of Ramadan is celebrated with particular fervor as commemorating the "Night of Power" (*laylat al-Qadr*) in which the Archangel Gabriel descended at God's command to bring the Koran to Muhammad.

In each family of means, charity is practiced extensively during the whole month and more particularly on the day of *'Īd al-fiṭr* which marks the end of the fast.

On that day, a special alms-giving, *zakāt al-fiṭr* is made obligatorily by all who have the necessary means. The whole city, now renewed and purified, rejoices for it recalls the inspired saying (*ḥadīth qudsī*) of the Prophet, by whose mouth God said: "The fast is for My sake and I reward him that fasts, for he foregoes for My sake his pleasure, food, and drink."

❧ *Alms-giving*

60. The dome treasury (*bayt al-māl*) in the court-yard of the great Umayyad Mosque, Damascus, Syria

The institution of prescribed alms-giving is literally a "purification" intended to attenuate or wipe out the attachment to material goods which tarnishes the heart, engages it in the accumulation of ephemeral riches, and engenders what Islam condemns as one of the most unforgivable of faults, namely: that of "associating" (*shirk*) other divinities with God, or as the most profound Islamic thinkers have understood it, of treating Truth and illusion on an equal footing, even preferring illusion to Truth.

Alms-giving (*zakāt*) reminds the believer that the enjoyment of his goods is only a temporary favor accorded him by God to test him: "Ye shall not attain to piety until ye give in alms what ye most love", says the Koran (3: 92).

Socially speaking, *zakāt* is an essential working—part of communal life. As the only "tax" demanded of believers by Koranic law, its amount is fixed, according to the nature of goods, at one tenth or one fifth of one's yearly gains as soon as these reach a fixed level. It is handed over to the Public Treasury which administers it and shares it out to those qualified to receive it, namely, poor and needy Muslims. It therefore ensures a certain redistribution of resources which, without seeking to equalize the inherent and predestined conditions of human fortune, imposes upon the rich a sacrifice that is to his profit and inspires feelings of gratitude in the poor, to whom God said: "Despair not of God's Goodness" (12: 87).

Over and beyond obligatory *zakāt*, voluntary alms-giving is strongly urged upon believers in the Koran and *Sunnah*. The Prophet is reported as saying: "Make no reckoning, for then God will make His reckoning with you; make no limits, for God will set limits against you; give in alms everything that you can!" This counsel has been very extensively followed and, as with the prescribed *zakāt*, voluntary *zakāt* has long served to help to meet the needs of the poor, to arm fighters in the Holy War, provision travelers, free slaves, redeem captives, and to assist the working of numerous institutions of religion and public utility.

Connected with the practise of *zakāt* and voluntary alms-giving is the institution of mortmain endowments (*waqf, ḥabūs*), given in perpetuity to the Muslim community for religious or public utility ends.

These pious foundations are amongst the most typical institutions of the Muslim city. Their origin is to be found in the *Sunnah*. According to a *hadīth* reported by Bukhāri, 'Umar once asked the Prophet how he could use, in a way agreeable to God, a piece of land he owned at Khaibar. The response was: "Make the property immovable, not subject to sale, gift, or inheritance and give its revenues to the poor." Thus was established the first *waqf*, the revenues of which were distributed to those deserving of *zakāt*.

Waqf is governed by three rules: 1. It is determined by the wish of the donor as expressed in the act of constitution, establishing the usage in perpetuity of the immobilized property; 2. It is not subject to any formality and can come about by a simple verbal declaration, providing that the donor is a responsible believer, that the donation is his property, and that it is not tarnished by any illegality; 3. Once engraved, the property is inalienable and inviolable. In this way, *waqf* has the effect of surrendering property to the ownership of God, whilst leaving the enjoyment of its benefits to His creatures.

Property assigned to *habūs* is of many kinds, movable and immovable. According to a list made in Morocco, the items given through religious endowments amount to about 40,000 objects: these include houses, shops, mills, bakehouses, baths, agricultural land, gardens, olive groves, single books or entire libraries, salt-pits, sections of water and conduits such as those leading from the wadi of Fez and the underground canal systems which supply the city of Marrakesh.[6]

61. *A Muslim Giving Alms*, Bustan of Sadi, Bihza, Persian miniature, 15th century

The institution of religious endowed property has rendered invaluable services to Muslim society. The administration of *habūs* has, down the centuries, assisted the working costs and, not infrequently, the construction of mosques, universities, sanctuaries, *zāwiyah*s, hospitals, asylums, and cemeteries. It has served to finance the building of city defenses, sanitation, and street lighting, the emoluments of judges and other religious functionaries, and to meet the personal wishes of the most diverse types as expressed by donors, such as feeding and caring for animals—asses, storks, or pigeons—providing drinking water in public markets, providing dowries for impoverished young women, etc. It demonstrates the zeal with which believers have applied the admonition to "expend in alms from that We have provided them" (8: 3), as well as the benefits the cities of Islam have drawn from it. "Whatever ye bestow in alms, God shall repay you. He is the Best Giver" (34: 39).

✧ *Pilgrimage*

No institution has contributed more than the Pilgrimage (*hajj*) to Mecca, Saudi Arabia, towards cementing the unity between believers in the worship of the One and Only God which is the *raison d'être* of the Muslim community and of each city of Islam.

The essential element of this rite, which each believer must perform at least once in his life, "if he has the means" (3: 97), is the flocking

6. J. Luccioni, 'Les habous au Maroc", conference held in Rabat on 20th January, 1928 (mimeographed document).

together around the Ka'bah of believers from all parts of the world, once a year on certain prescribed days.

The Ka'bah, which is the cube-shaped temple erected by Abraham to thank his Lord for sparing his son Isaac from the sacrifice to which he had been vowed and for whom a ram was substituted, is not only the center of the Muslim world; it is the point where Islam converges with the Abrahamic line, the entire preceding prophetic tradition of Judaism and Christianity, of which Muhammad appears as the inheritor and restorer. It is "God's House" on earth, on which the emanations of Heaven pour down and where a link operates between the finite and the Infinite. In deciding to visit Mecca, to which he has so often turned in prayer, the believer calls to mind the saying of the Prophet, that "the Pilgrimage performed in piety will have no other reward than Paradise". He formulates his intention to perform the Pilgrimage "for God alone", for the reward of any deed depends upon the intention that inspires it and, together with the blessings and prayers of his familiars, he bears with him piety "which is the best provision on the way" (Koran 2: 197). On arriving at his first destination, which is the point of entry to the Sacred Territory he is immediately caught up in a series of ceremonies that proceed without interruption for four days.

Simply by reviewing, even very summarily, the main components of the *hajj*, we shall see how each element combines to achieve a return

62. The door of the Ka'bah

63. The Ka'bah, Mecca, Saudi Arabia

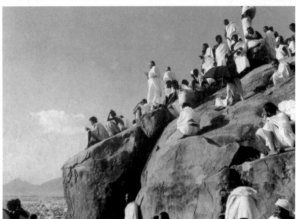

towards Unity as much through the modalities of earthly existence as in the heavenly dimension which finally integrates them:

⮑ historical unity, because the time of Abraham is made present and his acts are repeated as also are those of his wife, Hagar, seeking water in the desert, and their son, Ismael, ancestor of the Arabs; it is in emulation of Abraham, "a pure believer" (*ḥanīf*, according to the Koran 2: 135) and "friend of God" (*khalīl Allāh* 4: 125) that a pilgrim obeys an eternal law in accepting the sacrifice of his attachments and earthly desires;

⮑ spatial unity, actualized by the coming together of members of a widespread community on the same sacred territory and by the communal prayer performed by the pilgrims arrayed in concentric circles around the Ka'bah;

⮑ unity in the sacred nature of the human restored to his Adamic purity and integrity by the rites of consecration in which the body is draped in two pieces of white cloth and which forbid him to soil his soul with fleshly pleasures;

⮑ the unity, finally, of hundreds of thousands of believers, men and women "created from a single soul" (4: 1) all equally "poor before God, Who is alone Rich and worthy of praise" (35: 15), having responded to the call of their Lord and raising their voices towards Heaven in the same cry of submission: "*Labbayka-Llahumma Labbayka*" ("At Thy service Lord, at Thy service!").

Different stages of the pilgrimage (*hajj*):
64. *Top left*: Jabal Rahmah (Mount of Mercy), Arafat, Saudi Arabia

65. *Top right*: Pilgrim tents in Arafat, Saudi Arabia

66. *Bottom left*: Pilgrims performing *sa'ai* (seven rounds in a defined mode) between the hilltops Safah and Marwah, Saudi Arabia

67. *Bottom right*: Pilgrims waiting for the sunset on Jabal Rahmah, Arafat, Saudi Arabia

The effectiveness of the *hajj* as a unifying force is not limited to the period in which the great collective ritual is unfolded at Mecca, nor to within the borders of the Sacred Territory. For the Muslim community, the Kaʿbah is like a heart to which the pilgrims flood to recharge their strength and from which they are sent forth replenished with purified intent and quickening influences. These exchanges are affected not only at this level, but also along the pilgrim routes, where many months may be spent in travel by pilgrims who halt along the way to visit holy places and to see their co-religionists of other lands.

The setting out of a pilgrim no less than his return are everywhere marked with celebrations which are an extension of the rite itself, and aim at radiating its beneficent influence unto the family and the whole city.[7] But it is by celebrating the Feast of Sacrifice, the fourth and last day of the Pilgrimage that the entire Muslim community most particularly shares in the rite of Pilgrimage. On that day, throughout the Muslim world, men come together in mid-morning to say the communal prayers of *ʿĪd al-Kabīr*, the "great feast" of the Muslim calendar. In imitation of the pilgrims foregathered in the valley of Mina to proceed to the slaughter of the sacrificial beasts, each head of family ritually kills a sheep or a camel whose flesh will be eaten at a communal meal to which the poor are always invited.

68. The main entrance to the Mosque of Mecca, Saudi Arabia

4—THE FUNCTIONS OF THE CITY

Between the Muslim, sanctified by his monotheist faith and the practice of its basic rites, and the community of believers, whose effective presence we may have already grasped through the description of these rites, religious Law weaves many bonds. One would be hard put to review each one of them in the context of this brief study, inasmuch as the very domain of their operation—the collective entity—is inevitably stamped with the mark of diversity and relativity. Even in its sources alone, which are the Koran and the Traditions of the Prophet, the material on social relations is very copious. Moreover, the cleavage between Sunnite and Shīʿite Islam, the constitution of schools of dogma and even more, the geographical extension of the Muslim peoples and their historical evolution have all meant that variations and fluctuations do appear, if not in matters of principle, at least in the interpretation and modalities of application of religious institutions. At different places and times, the normative strength of certain rules is noted and reinforced or, on the contrary, relegated to the position of a simple, preferred option, or even a lapsed option.

But here again we must review fairly rapidly the principal functions, all devolving from religious ends, to which it is the mission of the Islamic city to respond. As regards the various bodies established for these ends, we shall simply sketch out their religious background in the knowledge that the form and content of political, juridical, economic, and social offices are set out in detail in a number of specialized books.

7. In certain communities of rural Morocco, a pilgrim back from Mecca is not considered a real *hajj* until he has performed a number of traditional practices such as a seven-day retreat in his house, visits to relatives and friends, visits to the tombs of saints protecting the village—cf. M. Boughali, *La Représentation de l'espace chez le marocain illettré* (Paris, 1974), 24 and 29.

69. The Prophet's Mosque, Medina, Saudi Arabia

✧ *Executive Power*

The Medina community, which was ordered to "obey God and His Prophet" (8: 1) since "he who obeyeth the Prophet obeyeth God" (4: 80), is the prototype of the Muslim Nation whose supreme leader is the Caliph, or imām, the Prophet's successor in whose person are united all the offices of spiritual authority and temporal power. His role is not to make laws, since Koranic Law is final and already promulgated, but to create the requisite conditions for fulfilling this law and guarding its application; it is an executive mandate which, being based upon legislation bestowed as an instrument of Divine Justice, has in addition judicial authority.

In order to guarantee the security of the lands under his sway, to lead the *jihād* on the frontiers, and to meet the needs of administration, the Caliph organizes his army and depends upon officials whom he posts to provinces and cities or appoints locally. The descriptions and titles of these officials have varied according to the period and the country; minister or vizier, governor, deputy, commander, tax-collector, pasha, etc. Their role is to maintain order in the city by creating a police force to protect it from external enemies, gather taxes and distribute revenue, and to run such public services as are not undertaken by religious foundations; thus it is a temporal role which, however, in a context where politics and religion are not disassociated, is played out

70. The Kutubiyyah Mosque, Marrakesh, Morocco

71. The Zaytuna Mosque and University, Tunis, Tunisia

according to norms imprinted with the religious mentality and which answers a duty of solidarity toward the community.

It is true that the preoccupation of the Umayyad Caliphate with affirming its political power and the subsequent transformation of the Caliphate into an autocratic kingship under the Abbassids, brought about an early cleavage between political/administrative functions on the one hand and juridical/religious ones on the other, which was further exacerbated by the fragmentation of the Muslim world into a multitude of autonomous entities. However, it was only with the introduction of national constitutions on the Western pattern and the abolition of the Ottoman Caliphate in 1924 that the final rupture came about between the executive power and religion in the greater part of *dār al-Islām*.

But this somewhat too schematic picture still needs certain qualifications; throughout history, the Caliphate or its equivalent, that is the authority of a virtuous leader enlightened in matters of religious knowledge and invested with power by Divine Decree—has always in Sunnite circles, been acclaimed by the doctors of the law as the sole form of legitimate government. There is no Muslim country that has not, at some period, been ruled by princes or dynasties ruling by virtue of this principle. Even today, there are a few Muslim states that have no official law other than the *sharī'ah*, under which they are governed. Others, despite their adoption of Western-type legislation, attempt to

72. Kasbah (fortress) of Ait Banhaddou, High Atlas, Morocco

73. The Bab Mellah, Fez, Morocco

make it conform—or at least not to conflict—with religious law, and for this purpose seek the counsel of traditional legal experts.

Thus it is that, curiously enough, political institutions in Sunnite Islam have evolved in a direction which brings them close to the position adopted by Twelve Imām Shī'ism more than a thousand years ago which, although it retired from the political scene with the occultation of the Imām al-Mahdī, has nonetheless continued to influence the behavior of temporal sovereigns and the conduct of state affairs by means of the opinions expressed by its learned men.

Such an attitude comes all the more naturally to Muslim awareness by being imbued with the notion that "the whole command belongeth to God" (13: 31). Thus God can exert His governance how He will and through whom He will. "Obey those among you that hold command" (4: 59) is how He orders believers, so that they are bound to recognize constituted authority as long as its holders do not openly contravene the precepts of revealed Law and providing that they accept, as far as their means and abilities allow, the duty to work for the establishment or restoration of the reign of the just Law of God in their city.

❧ *Judicial Authority*

The notion of justice is fundamental to Islam. The realm of Islam (*dār al-Islām*) is also called the "realm of justice" (*dār al-'adl*) because the Law that prevails there is that of God "the Just" (*al-'Adl*).

All the obligations and prohibitions of the religious law, *sharī'ah*, as well as the virtues which are, for the believer, the corollary and result of his submission to the Will and Wisdom of the Divine Legislator, come back to the same thing which is summarized in the classical formulae of jurisprudence: "give to each his due" or, more explicitly, "respect the rights of God and the rights of men".

Thus every function of the city is organized around a contractual relationship, the original pact whereby God placed man on earth as His vicegerent and which man agreed to in accepting this mission: the duty of the holders of authority to be protectors, which is matched by the duty of obedience to them on the part of subjects; and contracts governing social and other transactions of the private law, whereby men pledge themselves to one another without ever losing sight of the sovereign prerogatives of Him who had established the status of all things before any human intervention.

The affinity between this concept and the Platonic vision of the just society is self-apparent. Therefore, when the philosopher al-Farābī in the 4th/10th century described the ideal of a virtuous city, it was as a Muslim no less than as a disciple of Platonism that he defined its ends and means: "to have men in this life and on this earth enjoy as far as possible the happiness and delights of the life to come by means of communal institutions founded on justice and fellowship".[8]

In order for the God-decreed order to prevail, the city must depend

74. The minaret of al-Siba'iyya Madrasa, Damascus, Syria

8. Quoted after M.A. Lahbabi, *Du clos à l'ouvert* (Casablanca, 1961), "Propos II, La Civilisation des Cités".

upon men who possess, apart from a deep knowledge of the sources and branches of religion, proven moral qualities that will guarantee their having a "feeling for what is fair". This quality was thus described in the Koran (4: 135): "Ye who believe: hold staunchly to what is fair, as God's witness, be it against yourselves, your parents, or near relations, whether it concern a rich man or a poor, for God is the true patron of the one as of the other. Follow not passion at the price of justice. And if ye evade or turn aside, know that God knoweth well what ye do."

At the city level judicial authority is vested in the judge (*qāḍī*) who is appointed by the Caliph or chief of the executive. His place is in the mosque, and he is frequently called upon to deliver the Friday sermon (*khutbah*). His domain is the *sharī'ah* and extends to all the Koranic prescriptions, whose application to specific cases must be ensured by him. He conducts both marriage and divorce, sees that wills are honored, and looks to the interests of orphans and the incompetent; above all, he judges disputes that are put to him and applies the punishments provided for in the Koran for public or private misdemeanors.

In order to base his verdicts on surer ground, the judge frequently consults the *muftī*, a legal counselor to whom he is bound to refer matters of jurisprudence in accordance with the duty placed upon the leader of the community to consult others (according to Koran 3: 159). Ever since, in Sunnite Islam, "the doors of *ijtihād* were closed", the *muftī* has based his decisions (*fatwā*) on precedents contained in works on jurisprudence; he does not pronounce judgment on an action, nor does he formulate either punishment or probation, but expounds the theoretical or practical rules on which it is based and determines their modalities.

Finally, the judge designates certain persons as formal witnesses to help him in his tasks, whose role is essential for administering oaths; like notaries, they record formal statements which they can reproduce accurately in a dispute or court case and they form a respected class within the Muslim bourgeoisie.[9]

75. The Gök Madrasa, Turkey

76. The Tilla Kari Madrasa, Samarkand, Uzbekistan

❧ *Religious Instruction*

The role assigned to officials of justice explains quite clearly why the training of scholars of law (*'ulamā'*, *fuqahā'*) from whose ranks these officials are necessarily drawn, has been exalted to the position of a "duty of sufficiency" for the community.

There is, in fact, no higher distinction for a Muslim than to be credited with knowledge, that is to say, with knowledge of revealed Law. "He whom God wishes well", said the Prophet, "He makes learned in matters of religion." And again: "A single scholar of Law (*faqīh*) has more strength against Satan than a thousand men applying themselves to worship." This means not of course, that a learned man can dispense with ritual practices, but that these practices, associated with an intelligent understanding of their significance, acquire an all but invincible

9. Cf. E. Tyan, *Histoire de l'organisation judiciaire en pays d'Islam*, 2 vols. (Paris, 1939 and 1943).

counter-force against temptations, errors, and emotional involvements; the strength *fuqahā'* acquire by their knowledge empowers them to "loosen and to bind" the contractual commitments of which the lives of citizens are woven.

The institutionalization of religious instruction by the establishment of the first universities, and later of students' colleges (*madrasa*) at the very period when the great "methods" of jurisprudence were inaugurated, must not be allowed to conceal an enduring and still living reality, namely, the spontaneous handing on of the Koran and *Sunnah*

78. *Left*: Courtyard of the Mustansiriya Madrasa, Baghdad, Iraq, founded in 1223 by the Abbasid Caliph al-Muntansir, the first theological school to house the four recognized schools of Islamic law

79. *Above*: The door of the Ince Minara Madrasa, Konya, Turkey

77. *Opposite*: Prayer hall of the Qarawiyyin Mosque, Fez, Morocco ; **80**. *Bottom left*: Chahar Bagh Madrasa, Isfahan, Iran; **81**. *Bottom right*: Char Minar, entrance to the Khalif Niyazkul Madrasa, Bukhara, Uzbekistan

82. Al-'Attarin Madrasa, Fez, Morocco; **83**. The Shirda Madrasa, Samarkand, Uzbekistan

84. Courtyard of al-Azhar Mosque and University, Cairo, Egypt

at all levels of society and stages of life. For the young child, the imbibing of the Divine Word begins at the Koran school where he may acquire the respected title of *hāfiz* if he manages to learn the whole Koran by heart. In the surroundings of his family and society, he attends religious lectures and hears stories from the life of the Prophet and his Companions. As soon as he is old enough to pray, he hears the exhortations of the *imām* in the mosque. Public instruction is given by *'ulamā'* nearly always unpaid, "in the path of God", in the town's mosques or *zāwiyah*s where an audience from all categories of society listens to lessons in Koranic exegesis, *hadīth*, theology, and even expositions of writings on mysticism, Sufism. Sufism refers to the interior, mystical, and esoteric dimension of Islam.

By perpetuating the gift whereby "God taught man what he had never known" (96: 5), religious instruction on a large and generous scale remains one of the most operative factors in the maintenance and survival of Islamic civilization. If the acquisition of the necessary knowledge for performing a religious/legal function requires very many years of assiduous study, for which the universities and *madrasa*s are eminently suitable, nevertheless there is no citizen of even average education who may not exercise a consultative role within the community, lead the prayers as an *imām* and, through his acquaintance with the precepts of Law, practice the Koranic injunction to "command goodness" in his own circle.

85. A Muslim school in Indonesia; **86.** Tuareg tent set up for a Koranic reading, Niger

~ *The Maintenance of Moral Standards and the Encouragement of Goodness*

87. Koranic school of the Ifentar tribe in Tassila, south Morocco

88. A child learning to read the Koran, Niger

"Command what is decent, forbid what is blameworthy": such is the rightful duty of a just man together with faith in God, whether he belong to "the upright community of the People of the Book" (according to Koran 3: 113-114) or to the community Muhammad was sent to (3: 104-110).

Every Muslim is bound, under the conditions defined by jurisprudence and, except in cases of *force majeure*, precluding the shedding of blood, to criticize and denounce public and private acts which are contrary to the limits set by God and if it be within his power, to rectify them in order to restore order in the community.

However, it is above all the moral aspect of this Koranic exhortation "to command goodness" by word of mouth and personal example which has, in city life, been retained as a duty of the individual, whereas the actual correction of misdemeanors has been treated as a collective responsibility. As such, it became the concern of the *qādī* and of another official appointed by him, the *muhtasib*, a very typical personality of the classical Muslim city.

As an official for the supervision of moral standards, social behav-

ior, and public security, the *muhtasib* kept an eye on the performance of such religious duties as Friday prayers or the Fast, on correct behavior between men and women on the streets, the safety of buildings, and the cleanliness of roads; he intervened at schools against teachers who mistreated their pupils, and prevented animal-owners from overloading beasts of burden. At market places and street stalls he supervised the honesty of commercial transactions and the manufacture of goods by craftsmen, rooted out fraud and imposture, and denounced exorbitant prices. To help him to check on the various professions, he appointed provosts of guilds to watch over the quality and fairness of services rendered to the clientele of their respective sectors.

This institution, which was considered a religious one, survived into the dawn of the modern age. Then it gradually died out as part of its functions were handed over to officials of the police or the municipal authorities, others to the *qādī*, and others simply became obsolete as the public became ever more intransigent to normal censure as being, partly under the influence of Western concepts, an intrusion on "the freedom of the individual".

The commanding of good and the forbidding of evil are inseparable from the very existence of the Muslim community, which is a body which suffers as a whole when even one of its members is sick, as we will recall from the *hadīth* quoted previously. The bond of fellowship or solidarity doubtless had strong roots in pre-Islamic Arab society in which it was one of the conditions of clan and tribal life. But it was Islam that gave it entirely fresh support and significance by extending it to the entirety of men and women who hold to the Message of the Koran.

Fellowship between believers did not result in the suppression of bonds as between fellow-tribesmen or members of a particular social milieu—the nobility of a kinship bond may well be outweighed by that conferred by piety but it is not thereby abolished—or in impeding the formation of new groupings based on ethnic, social, professional, or other affinities. On the contrary, it would seem that adherence to a common faith was actually favorable to the establishment of very varied types of associations throughout the world of Islam. Although certain of these have contributed to emphasizing the particular nature of specific groups and others have even degenerated into factions and caused serious disturbances within cities,[10] others have succeeded in extracting ethical concepts of truly universal relevance from the teachings of Islam. Such were the knightly orders (the Eastern *futuwwāt* and the *murābitun* of the Maghreb) and the professional guilds before they too suffered a decline like that of moral standards.[11] And such were, *par excellence*, the Sufi brotherhoods (*tarīqah*, plural: *turuq*) which grew up in the first cities of Islam—Basrah, Kufah, and Baghdad—and which played a considerable part in Islam's expansion (notably) to India, Malaysia, and large parts of Africa, and whose radiation has retained in our own day an indisputable vitality. The sanctifying influence exerted by the "friends of God" and the "poor in God" (*fuqarā'*) or dervishes of Islam

89. Tile work from the *mihrāb* of the Wazi Khan Mosque, Lahore, Pakistan

10. The part played in this respect by certain groups, militia, and *ahdāth* in Syria, *'ayyārūn* and *fityān* in Iraq and Iran, has been elucidated by Cl. Cahen, "Mouvements populaires et autonomisme urbain dans l'Asie musulmane du moyen age" in *ARABICA*, V, 3 (1958) and VI, 1 and 3 (1959). See also *E.I (2)*, article *FUTUWWA* edited by the same author and Fr. Taeschner.

11. In this context, we should note the opinion of L. Massignon who wrote in 1924: "If these guilds fade away . . . the entire social life of towns is threatened with regression". "Enquête sur les corporations musulmanes au Maroc", *Rev. Monde Mus.*, vol. LVIII, 82.

on the mentality and manners of the city would itself deserve a special study and can only be briefly noted here.[12]

EPILOGUE

Much more would need to be said to complete this all-too-brief outline of the religious institutions of the Islamic city. In particular, we should dwell a little upon the basic cell of the city which is the family, and bring out its functional hierarchy which, by divine Decree, establishes its patriarchal nature: the authority of the father or grandfather over the family as a whole; the respect and kindness owed by believers to their parents and, especially, to the mother who "bore him in pain and brought him forth with pain" (46: 15). Men and women are fundamentally equal in their spiritual nature, even though their rights correspond to their different fucntions in society—for are not men and women "created from a single soul" (4: 1)?—nor their status as believers whereby they are bound to the same devotional duties to God as are men and promised the same rewards in the Hereafter.

Nor should one overlook consideration of the subtle web of convention drawn from the Koran and the *Sunnah* whereby Muslim personality displays itself at both the individual and collective levels: the rules of politeness comprising all the gestures, attitudes, and words used by Muslims on meeting: congratulations on happy occasions, consolation in life's trials, calling upon God as witness to their common dependence upon the Almighty and hoping for His Infinite Mercy for one another; and good behavior towards God which includes the wearing of traditional garments and headwear, the turban being the symbol *par excellence* of the believer's dignity and his alliance with Heaven, no less than the utterance of certain Koranic formulae such as *in shā'Allāh*— "If God will!", whereby the servant announces an intention without forgetting that all things are decreed by God; the *basmalah*—"in the Name of God", and the *hamdalah*—"praise God!"—whereby a believer initiates and concludes his actions, accepting that it is God alone who orders all things and dispenses all benefits.

From these observations—we realize that religious institutions are a kind of matrix—we have used the simile of a pyramid and its edges—within which Muslim personality is positively enwrapped in the recollection of divine Unity.

This is why no enumeration, however detailed, of the precepts and regulations of religious Law could possibly exhaust the contents of Muslim life. Within the institutional framework which shapes it, there are transformations and syntheses at work—a veritable spiritual alchemy which owes everything to Islam but transcends its strictly normative aspects.

To be convinced of this, it is enough to consider the products of Islamic art which transmit a vision of reality—and one that is homogeneous, original, and always true to itself through time and

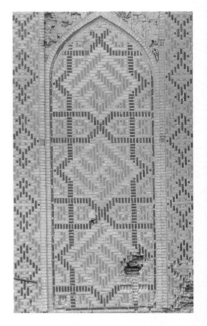

90. Inscription of the Divine Name, *Allāh*, in Kufic style on the facade of Bibi Khanum Mosque, Samarkand, Uzbekistan

12. Fine examples of this for the saints of the first centuries of the Hegira dwelling in Basrah, Kufah, and Baghdad are given in: E. Dermenghem, *Vies des Saints musulmans*, new ed. (Algiers S.D.) and for a contemporary Muslim city in T. Burckhardt, *Fez: City of Islam* (Cambridge U.K.: The Islamic Texts Society, 1992).

space—which neither the rites of religion nor the prescriptions of law and jurisprudence have ever undertaken to define specifically; or to ponder the teachings and writings bequeathed to us by Muslim thinkers and mystics—the philosophical and metaphysical legacy of such men as Ibn Sīnā, Ibn ʿArabī, or Mullā Sadrā, or the songs of divine love of Ibn al-Fārid, Rūmī, and other Sufis without number.

The fact is that the revealed Message has two dimensions or aspects: one that is outward and on the surface and another that is inward and deep. The first is the Law (*sharīʿah*) which is binding on all responsible men and women, ties them to itself by reason, and rules their faculties of feeling and action; followed to the letter, it makes for the restoration to creatures of their original status and shapes them to attain to the felicity promised in the Hereafter. The second is Truth (*haqīqah*) which concerns the essential realities hidden behind outward appearances and is perceptible only to the "eye of the heart" open to contemplation. It is like the anticipation in this world of the vision God accords to His intimates.

The Islamic community has, from the beginning, acknowledged the existence of a hierarchy of spiritual qualifications in its members, a gradation based not on any social or external criteria but on the degree of a man's absorption in his religion. As in the terminology of the famous "*hadīth* of Gabriel", one speaks of three categories of the faithful: the *muslim* who conforms to the five pillars of religion, the *muʾmin* ("believer") who adheres to sincere faith in the revealed truths, and the *muhsin* ("virtuous") who adores God as if he saw Him, "for if you don't see Him, He sees you!"

Knowing that its destiny is to have men live consciously beneath the eye of God in order that each may receive his due portion of the Light and Mercy for which he is destined, the Islamic city has long striven to preserve its institutions as the providential means of this flowering. And it is a fact that the contemplative potentialities which Islam bears in itself have never been expressed with such vigor in art, philosophy, and mysticism as during the periods when the *sharīʿah* was the great Law of the city.

These periods appear to be a thing of the past. After taking over political institutions, secularization has spread to the realms of public and private law, education, fiscal practice, and the judiciary. Today, the unity of the Muslim community is more than ever compromised by national rivalries and ideological dissensions which rarely have anything to do with the ultimate interests of believers.

How should the city react to the challenge of the present and yet remain Muslim? I am certainly not qualified to answer a question which has for a long time caused much spilling of ink and much preoccupation to many good minds. One can only express the fervent hope that, when they are instituted, the long awaited and necessary reforms will be in the spirit of Islam, and trust that the religious institutions which have just been described—intangible "pillars of Islam" on the one hand, and functions of the community on the other, firm in their principles but open to variations and adaptations in their actual application—may continue to act as strong guides and sources of inspiration for those who are striving to preserve the salvational role of the city:

> Only they that are endowed with perception shall ponder; who fulfill God's Pact and break not the Covenant; who join together that which God hath commanded to be joined; who fear their Lord and are in awe of the evil of the Reckoning; who are patient in seeking the face of their Lord, establish the prayer, and give in charity of that wherewith We have provided them, secretly and openly, and return good for evil; it is to these that the last dwelling place is given, Gardens of Eden....
>
> (Koran 13: 19-23)

91. *Opposite:* Tile work detail from Morocco

92. The Generalife Gardens, Alhambra, Granada, Spain

93. *Top*: The Shah Mosque, Isfahan, Iran; **94**. *Bottom left*: Ksar Goulmina, a fortress in Morocco;
95. *Bottom right*: The Aljafería Palace, Zaragoza, Spain

PART II

THE MESSAGE OF ISLAMIC ART

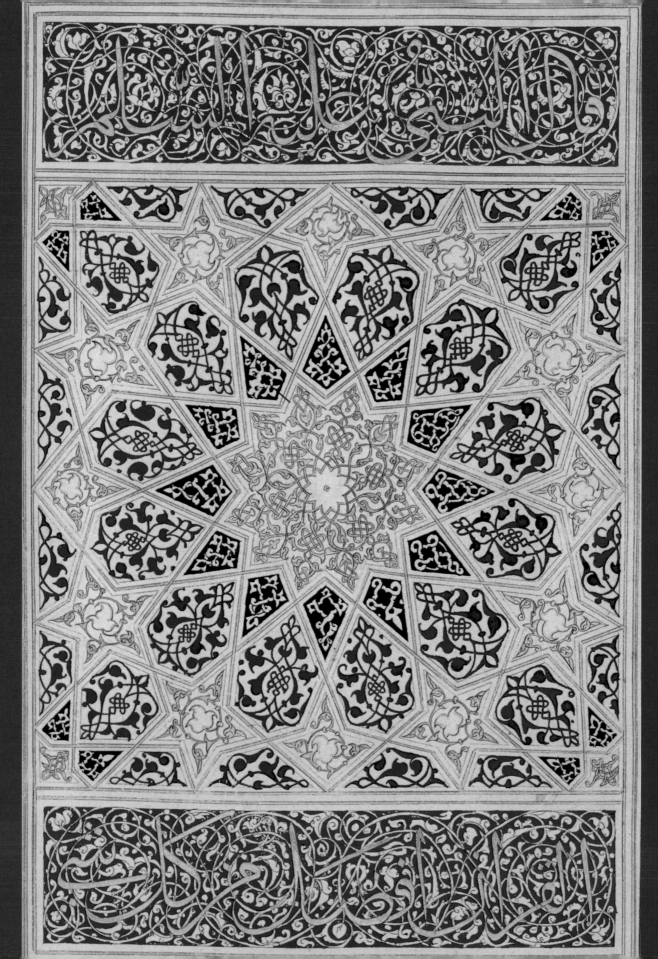

PART II

THE MESSAGE OF ISLAMIC ART

Read: in the Name of thy Lord Who createth,
Createth man from a clot,
Read: And it is thy Lord the Most Bountiful
Who teacheth by the pen,
Teacheth man that which he knew not.
(Koran 96: 1-5)

It was with this summons, this command given to the Prophet Muhammad by the archangel Gabriel that the Koranic Revelation opened fourteen centuries ago in 612 AD, ten years before the start of the Hegira. And this same summons which exhorted Muhammad to read aloud, to proclaim the Divine Message is, it seems to me, well suited to introduce an exposition on the subject of which is the art of Islam.

This is so not only because these verses of the Koran were the first to be revealed, thus marking the beginning of the great adventure of Islam, but equally for more precise reasons, because with these first words of the Sacred Book, with what they say and with the form in which they say it, the art of Islam is already present.

96. *Opposite*: Koran illuminated by 'Abd Allāh ibn Muhammad al-Hamadānī for the Sultan Ūlljaytū, 713/1313, frontispiece to part 28, ff. 1v-2r, Hamadan, Iran

97. *Below*: Anonymous Koran, Ottoman Empire, c. 1750-1800

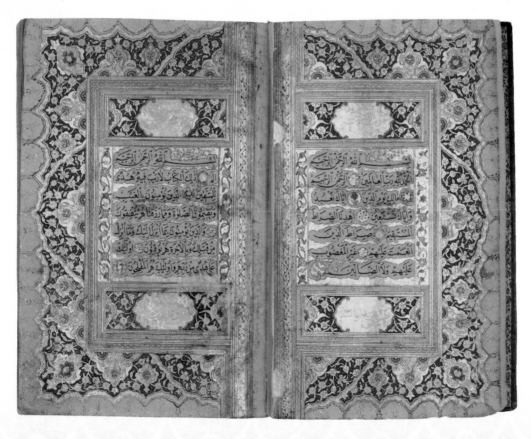

These words, as said in Arabic, have a very precise resonance, an intrinsic force which is linked to, among other things, the principal meanings of the following triliteral roots and the alliterations and permutations of letters which they give rise to: Kh-L-Q—to create and '-L-Q—the clot; Q-R-'—to read and Q-L-M—the pen or calamus; '-L-M—to know, recognize and again Q-L-M, the calamus.

In short the Koran, which as its name in Arabic suggests, is the "reading", the "recitation" *par excellence*, given to be heard, memorized, and repeated in full, carries within itself the roots of the first art of Islam which is recitation of the Koran in Arabic. And because the words of the Revelation are assembled in a Book and are composed of letters we have already in embryo the second major art of Islam which is calligraphy, an art which man carries within himself, in a certain manner, from the beginning of the Revelation since "God teacheth man by the pen", the calamus or reed, a symbol of the Prime Intellect, which, having been plunged in the ink of divine Wisdom traces the sacred signs which grant the human being access to knowledge.

Recitation, the art which manifests the sound and modulations in Arabic of the verses of the Koran in time; calligraphy, the art which transcribes visually the vocables and fixes them in space … with these two modes of expression we find ourselves at the very source of the art of the Muslims, the source from which the artists of Islam have never ceased over the centuries to draw their inspiration.

Specialists in Islamic art usually approach their subject from an angle that is both chronological and geographical; they describe its evolution in time, analyze the borrowings and original contributions, point out the individuality of works created at different periods, in the various parts of the Islamic world and in the various spheres of application: architecture, music, the industrial and decorative arts. Such an approach is evidently inappropriate in the frame of a concise essay, where it would only lead to a tedious enumeration of places, art works, and patrons. Besides, the analytical character of such an approach would hardly allow it to set in relief the characteristics and permanent values of Islamic art which enable the latter, everywhere and at all times, to be true to itself and confer on it an incontestable originality.

That is why I deemed it important to consider Islamic art from another point of view that is neither historical nor descriptive but which is based on what one could call the "spiritual universe" of Islam. Without doubt this universe is not the property of artists alone. Being that of the revealed Message, it belongs to every Muslim. But as soon as the artist intervenes, the ideas which he entertains are transferred to the material objects which become the common property of the community. Hence the necessity of knowing the meaning of these ideas if one wishes to be able the better to read and understand the language into which they are transcribed.

98. The Suleymaniye Mosque, Istanbul, Turkey

99. "Verily in the remembrance of *Allāh* do hearts find rest" (*'alā bi-dhikri-Llāhi tatma'innu 'l-qulūb*) (Koran 13: 28); calligraphy by Shahriar Piroozram

1—ART: AN INTEGRAL PART OF MUSLIM LIFE

In the Koran, God says, in speaking of man, "I created him only that he might worship Me" (51: 56). Further, it is said, "Nothing is greater than the remembrance of God!" (29: 45). It follows then that the real *raison d'être* of man is to worship God, which implies that the whole of his existence should be an act of devotion and remembrance vis-a-vis his Maker.

The idea of remembrance, of recollection—*dhikr, tadhkīr*—is fundamental to Islam. The Koran is called *dhikr Allāh*, remembrance of God, and *dhikr Allāh* is also one of the names given to the Prophet Muhammad, not only because he was the trustee and transmitter of the Koran, but also because his behavior, his words, and his teachings—in short all that makes up the *Sunnah*, the Prophetic Tradition—show to what extent he remembered his Lord, and as a result of this constant remembrance, was near to Him.

This preoccupation, this obsession one might even say, with the recollection, the remembrance of God is not only a factor in individual perfection. It is also a stimulating ferment to social life and artistic development. In order to remember God often, it is necessary in effect that the members of the Muslim community should contrive to surround themselves at every moment of their lives—and not only during the ritual prayer—with an ambiance favorable to this remembrance. Such an ambiance would need to be beautiful and serene so that the human beings one met as well as all the things, natural or artificial one encountered, could become the occasion for and the support of the *dhikr* (remembrance of God).

With regard to the human and social milieu, such an ambiance is realized through the practice of the *sharī'ah*, the revealed religious Law which contains the rules to which all are obliged to conform. Thanks to this law, the five essential pillars of Islam, a network of sacralized behavior patterns, as much individual as collective, is woven into the heart of the collectivity, the *ummah*.

As to the imprint given to the material environment so that it too might become a mirror of the spiritual world, it is here, precisely, that one enters the domain of art, of sacred art which, according to the words of the contemporary *Maitre a penser* Frithjof Schuon, "is first of all the visible and audible form of Revelation and then also its indispensable liturgical vesture".[1]

The function of artists consists in translating the principles of Islam into aesthetic language, in other words, transposing them into forms and motifs which will be incorporated into the structures and used in the decoration of all things from sanctuaries and palaces to the most humble domestic utensil. "God is beautiful; He loves beauty", says a *hadīth*[2] which could be regarded as the doctrinal foundation of Muslim aesthetics.

100. A calligrapher in Tunis, Tunisia

101. *Hadith*: "Verily God is beautiful; He loves beauty" (*Inna'Llāhu jamīl yuhibbu'l-jamāl*); calligraphy by Shahriar Piroozram

1. F. Schuon, *Understanding Islam*, trans. from French by D.M. Matheson (London: Allen & Unwin, 1963, 1976, 1979; Baltimore, Maryland: Penguin Books, 1972), chap. 4.

2. Imam Ahmad, *Musnad*.

According to the Islamic perspective, which underlines the absolute supremacy of the rights of the Creator over those of the creature, artistic creativity is nothing other than a predisposition which God has placed in man to help him follow the path which leads to Him. The artist is therefore only one among others of the servants of God; he does not belong to any exceptional category. He should himself, the better to fulfill his role in the collectivity, become, by means of effacement and disinterested service, an as transparent as possible interpreter of the Tradition to which he subscribes. Whence the relationship that has always existed with Muslim artists between the practice of virtues and the excellence of professional work. The Prophet said: "God loves that when one of you does something, he does it thoroughly." And one can confirm that this advice has been followed to the letter, in particular by the artisans of the guilds and brotherhoods of the entire classical period for whom the artisanal pact was a unanimously respected professional code of honor.

Another characteristic of artistic creativity in Islam is that it is never exercised "gratuitously", by which we are to understand that it always answers to well-defined ends. Unlike the art of the modern West, Islamic art has never known the distinction between an art supposedly "pure", or "art for art's sake", and a utilitarian or applied art, the first aiming solely at provoking an aesthetic emotion and the second supposedly responding to some need. In fact, Islamic art is always "functional", that is to say useful, whether the utility is directly of the spiritual order—like the Koranic verses engraved on the pediment of a mausoleum or embroidered on the veil which covers the Ka'bah at Mecca—or whether it pertains to many levels at the same time, as with a chandelier or a bronze basin inlaid with arabesques.

102. *Top left*: Detail of a *kiswah* (embroidered black cloth which covers the Ka'bah)

103. *Bottom left*: Inscriptions on the crypt of the Qutub Minar, Delhi, India

104. *Center*: Brass lamp from Isfahan, Iran

105. *Center right*: Engraved washbowl from the Timurid period, Iran

It will perhaps be noticed that I use the terms "artist" and "artisan" without distinction to designate those who are responsible for the artistic expression of Islam. This is because in classical Arabic there is only one word to indicate the man who works and fashions with his hands; it is *sāni*, the artisan, someone who practices a craft or trade, for which he must serve an apprenticeship in a technique, in an "art"—in the sense in which this term was used in the Middle Ages, and not in the modern world. The Arabic word *fann* (art) carries the same ancient connotation. This meaning is found expressed, notably, in the adage *ars sine scientia nihil*, "technique (or skill) without knowledge (or wisdom) counts for nothing"—an adage Muslim artisans could have made their own and of which, it may be said in passing, our modern technocrats would do well to take note. Therefore, the artist, as we know him today, with his search after individual expression and his rather marginal position in society does not exist in the world of traditional Islam which is what we are now concerned with and that is why the use of either term, "artist" or "artisan", should not lend itself in this context to any misunderstanding.

There are, no doubt, some crafts which by their nature do not give rise to obvious artistic products. Certain professional specialties, like the tanning of skins, the carding or the dyeing of wool, cannot, however, be detached from the process of production the final product of which—a ceremonial saddle or a carpet—will be a work of art. On the other hand, certain artistic elements—for example the work songs or the badges and special costumes worn on the feast days of the guilds are nearly always associated with the practice of the traditional crafts and constitute a not inconsiderable contribution to the cultural life of Muslim society.

In brief, there are two essential characteristics of Islamic artistic production. Firstly: from the spiritual and ethical point of view, it derives essentially from the Koranic Message, the values of which it aims to translate onto the formal plane. Secondly: from the technical point of view, it rests on the transmission from father to son, or master to apprentice, of unchangeable rules and practices. Such a transmission does not in any way imply stagnation and the automatic repetition of earlier designs. On the contrary, at most times, it has assured a constant source of inspiration to the artists and a stability on the technical level

106. Tannery in the old quarter of Fez, Morocco

107. The city of Fez in Morocco has some 150 caravanserais (*fondouk*), which may serve as a hostel for travelers (and a stable for their mounts), a storeroom for merchandise, a workshop for craftsmen, and as a trading center. Some, like the Fondouk Sagha, built in 1749-50, are of fine architectural quality

which have favored the creation of numerous masterpieces that are in no way repetitive. If, at other times, the ancient formulae have become somewhat exhausted as a result of being reproduced, it is necessary to look elsewhere than in the formulae themselves for the cause of this decadence.

2—THE FORMAL LANGUAGES

In a way similar to what happened with the birth of the cities, the time required by the art of Islam to fully develop its personality was relatively very short. It extended over the first 150 odd years after the death of the Prophet (in the 10th year of the Hegira or 632 of the Christian era) and coincided with the lightning-like expansion of Islam across the Asiatic and Mediterranean worlds as well as with the first decades of the establishment of the Abbasid Caliphate at Baghdad (750 AD).

This growth was the result of contact with the old cultures which Islam encountered and subjugated. Placed at its disposal were the techniques and artistic forms practiced by various civilizations, the Hellenistic (and Romano-Byzantine) of Syria, the Sassanid of Persia and Mesopotamia, the Coptic of Egypt (with its Pharaonic heritage), without mentioning the numerous local traditions like those of the Berbers of North Africa or of the Visigoths of Spain, which Islam was able to sweep along in its wake.

All these pre-existing elements were placed at the service of the new community. Often their original forms remained intact, at least to begin with, after which a selection was operated as much by the artists themselves, many of whom were converts to Islam and thus obedient to the new ethical and aesthetic criteria, as by reason of new needs to which art would henceforward have to comply. Amongst these needs those of worship played a predominant role and it was in religious architecture that Islamic art first manifested its faculty for integrating pre-existing artistic traditions and adapting them to its own vision and needs. In order to grasp in what sense this evolution took place, let us take the classical example of the Grand Mosque of Damascus which was constructed by the Umayyads at the end of the 7th century AD. At the time of construction, the Byzantine artists summoned to execute the glass mosaics on the facades of the court and the walls of the portico used a style of decor (fig. 108)—with thick-leafed trees and architectural elements done in *trompe l'oeil*—which was fashionable in the Eastern part of the Roman Empire and still reflected the naturalistic tradition of Rome and Greece. The remarkable fact is that naturalistic motifs like these did not appear subsequently in religious monuments, whereas the geometric and vegetal elements of these same mosaics— i.e. double spirals, rosettes, foliage, and garlands—were retained and soon developed in refined compositions (as on the *mihrāb* of Córdoba, scarcely a century later). (fig. 109)

108. *Top*: Mosaic from the Great Mosque of Damascus, Syria

109. *Bottom*: Mosaics from the *mihrāb* of the Great Mosque of Córdoba, Spain

In similar vein, the frescoes of the "desert palaces", those country-seats built for the Umayyad Caliphs, contain numerous representations of human beings: musicians, dancers, hunters, executed in the Hellenistic or Sassanid style. This art of the figurative fresco was abandoned fairly quickly and hardly ever re-appeared except in the form, greatly reduced in size, of the miniature.

These examples could be multiplied, but what concerns us above all is to see according to what criteria this selection was operated. The major criterion, which I believe to have already suggested, is the power each work of art should have to recall the Divine Unity, to suggest it in some way, and in all cases not to distract the attention and senses to the extent that the viewer becomes captivated by illusory appearances. Art should help the soul to concentrate on the essential and not turn it towards the accidental and the transitory.

It is moreover in this preoccupation that one should see the deep-rooted reason for the rejection of figurative representation in Islamic art. This refusal is not founded upon a legal prohibition inscribed in the Koran; but it expresses a repugnance at seeing man substitute himself for the Creator in wishing to imitate natural forms. In itself the creative act of the artist is not reprehensible, quite the contrary, since God Himself in the Koran, uses the example of the potter who molds clay to characterize His own creative act:

He created man of clay like the potter (Koran 55: 14).

But such an act runs the risk of engendering in the human artist the illusion of having himself added something to the creation, whence the temptation to pride, which in Islam is considered to be the worst sin of all, since it tends to place the creature at the level of the Creator, or in other terms, to ascribe to God an equal or an associate. Equally, figurative art may have the effect on the observer of making him admire the human genius who, instead of revealing in his work the infinite richness of Him Who created the prototypes of all things, knows how to reproduce a tree, a flower, or the human body in its physical appearance.

Whence the systematic preference of Islamic art for impersonal, linear forms which have a geometrical or mathematical basis. Such is the case with the two forms of art which, as we have seen before, were "given" by the Revelation: recitation of the Koran in Arabic and calligraphy.

The recitation of the Koran is the sacred art *par excellence*. "God has never sent a prophet without giving him a beautiful voice", declared the Prophet Muhammad, and the history of the Koranic revelation illustrates the pertinence of this remark. Brought to men "in a clear, Arabic tongue" (according to Koran 26: 195), the divine Message had to be proclaimed clearly. "Chant the Koran very distinctly!" was the command given to Muhammad (Koran 73: 4); and he himself, in a

110. *Top*: Brick inscription, Friday Mosque, Isfahan, Iran

111. *Center*: Wall decoration in glazed earthenware (*zellij*), Fez, Morocco

112. *Bottom*: Earthenware mosaic, Chah-i-Zindeh, Samarkand, Uzbekistan

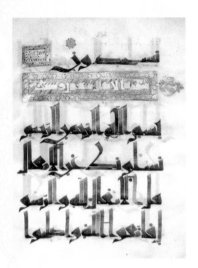

113. Page from an Eastern Kufic Koran, Koufa, Iraq, 11th century

3. There are seven or, according to certain classifications, ten schools of readings of the Koran which all go back to the 2nd century of the Hegira and are drawn from the prophetic tradition. They are as follows:

1) The School of Medina, founded by Nāfi' (d. 169/785) whose principal disciple was the Imām Malik. Spread into Egypt, Tunisia, Sicily, Algeria, and Spain;

2) The School of Mecca, founded by Ibn Kathīr (d. 120/738);

3) The School of Basrah, founded by Ibn al-'Alā (d. 154/771);

4) The School of Damascus, founded by Ibn 'Āmir (d. 118/736) and still widely practiced in Syria;

5) The School of Kufah, which itself is comprised of three branches; they are:

a) the School of 'Asim al-Asadī (d. 128/745) spread throughout the Muslim world and today firmly implanted in Egypt thanks to the recent editions of the Koran;

b) the School of Hamza al-Ijlī (d. 156/772), propagated in Morocco; and

c) the School of Kisā'ī (d. 189/805) of which Ibn Hanbal was a zealous defender and which is still popular in Eastern Arabia and in Iraq (cf. Muhammad Tāhir al-Khattāt, *Ta'rikh al-Qur'ān* [Cairo, 2nd ed. 1372/1953], 108; and Si Hamza Boubakeur, see following note.)

4. *Hadīth* cited by Si Hamza Boubakeur, "La psalmodie coranique", in *Encylopédie des Musiques sacrées*, I (Paris), 388.

hadīth, recommended to the faithful, "Embellish your voices with the Koran, and embellish the Koran with your voices", giving to mean that there exists a veritable consubstantiality between the divine Word and the human voice. To read, to recite the Koran in Arabic, is in effect and in the most direct way, to let oneself be penetrated by the divine Word, to become imbued with its significance and its vibration; it is, for each believer, to approach the Divine, to live in the Presence, to taste the Names and the Qualities before, perhaps, having a presentiment of the Essence.

In the same way that the Koran cannot be compared to any other literary production, likewise psalmody, which constitutes the first sacred art of Islam, is necessarily distinguished from all other musical expression. Its unique character is reflected in its terminology, since the terms by which it is designated borrow nothing from musical vocabulary, terms such as *qirā'a*, reading, *tartīl* or *tilāwa*, psalmody, *tajwīd*, from the root *jwd*, embellish; but never *ghinā'*, song, vocal music. It should not include any element of individual creation apt to denature an intangible text, and the only concern of the reciter should be to efface himself before the divine model and to conform himself to it as thoroughly as possible.

It ensues that psalmody obeys precise rules which, if they vary in detail according to different schools, nevertheless rest on common principles.[3] In the first place, given that the Divine Book contains in itself its own rhythm, its reading never allows for any instrument of accompaniment. It is incumbent upon the reciter to render the rhythmic structure perceptible by giving a correct pronunciation, by respecting the lengthening of vowels and redoubling of consonants, by making the traditional pauses and breaks, these latter having the special function of retaining the attention, of letting the imagination work, and of facilitating the assimilation of the meaning of the verses.

As for the melodic element, it can be totally dismissed, as one of the juridical schools of Sunnism, that of the Imām Malik, wished, without losing any of the vibratory effect. It suffices to listen to the collective reading as it is practiced in the mosques of Morocco to be convinced of the power of penetration of a recitation done *recto tono*. Most generally however, the systems of reading teach a kind of more or less rapid cantillation, the modulation of which spans a variable but generally narrow register, and which underlines and embellishes the syllables and the words by means of melismas and vocalizations so as to engrave them more easily on the human substance.

"Recite the Koran following the melodies and the intonations of the Arabs", the Prophet was to advise.[4] That this injunction was generally followed is demonstrated by the undeniable kinship that exists among all the styles of psalmody in the Muslim world. It is true that in the course of its expansion in space, the art of psalmody has absorbed a number of melodic elements present in the local milieu, and it is that which gives birth to easily recognizable, characteristic styles. All these styles, however, bear the indelible stamp of Islam; they incorporate a unique sonorous substance which itself has served as a vehicle of the Koranic Message.

Psalmody is practiced on all occasions, individually or collectively. It is for each believer the means *par excellence* of remembering God and of meditating on His Qualities and blessings following His injunction: "Surely in the creation of the heavens and earth and in the alternation of night and day there are signs for men possessed of minds who remember God, standing and sitting and on their sides, and reflect upon the creation of the heavens and the earth (and say): 'Our Lord, Thou hast not created this for vanity. Glory be to Thee! Guard us against the chastisement of the Fire!'" (Koran 3: 190-191). Taught to children from the earliest age, it not only impresses upon them the spiritual and moral teachings of Islam, but it acts upon the very fibers of their sensibility and works, through the alchemy of the Word, a transmutation which restores to the human creature something of its primordial sacredness.

From psalmody are derived numerous manifestations of religious life, such as the call to prayer, the liturgical recitation of litanies, and the intoning of *mawladiyyāt* (songs celebrating the birthday of the Prophet Muhammad) and mystical poems. No less important is the influence of psalmody on the whole of Arab music, including instrumental music, whether it concerns religious music—such as that which is played at the meetings of the mystical brotherhoods—or profane music, the demarcation between the two types being moreover often difficult to establish. There lies, however, such an important field of the artistic creativity amidst the Muslim world that it will be necessary to deal with it in greater detail at a later stage.

As to calligraphy, its role is equally to make perceptible the eternal beauty of the Koran. After having served to establish, some twenty years after the death of the Prophet, a complete and definitive version of the Book, it has never ceased to spread the text, giving birth to forms and styles of writing the aesthetic qualities of which arouse the admiration even of non-Muslims and non-Arabists.

Each script, in playing on the forms, dimensions, and proportions of the letters, brings more particularly into relief certain divine Attributes. Thus the divine Majesty, Rigor, and Transcendence are evoked by the vertical strokes, especially that of the *alif*, the symbol of the Unity of the Supreme Principle which stamps its mark on the rhythms of the discourse. Beauty, Gentleness, and Immanence are expressed by the horizontal lines, above and below which are written the diacritic and vowel signs, like the notes of a musical score. Finally Perfection and Plenitude are suggested by the rounded forms, such as the *nun* for example in the style of the Maghrib.[5]

114. Page from a Maghrebi Koran, 13th century

5. The way in which calligraphy has been applied to buildings and objects composing the Islamic environment is well illustrated in A. Welch, *Calligraphy in the Arts of the Muslim World*, catalogue of an exhibition held at Asia House Gallery, Asia Society, New York during the winter of 1979, containing a good bibliography on the subject.

The variety of calligraphic styles used throughout time and space for the transcription of the Koran is beautifully illustrated in M. Lings, *Splendors of Qur'an Calligraphy and Illumination* (Liechtenstein: Thesaurus Islamicus Foundation, 2005).

For an analysis in depth of the role played by calligraphy in the Islamic culture and its relationship with Sufism, see A. Schimmel, *Calligraphy and Islamic Culture* (London: I.B. Tauris & Co., 1990).

Left: Letter *alif*; *right*: letter *nun*

115. Frontispiece of an illuminated Mamluk Koran, Cairo, Egypt, 14th century; **116.** Tile work from the Alhambra, Granada, Spain; **117.** Tile work on the ceiling of the Chahar Bhag Madrasa, Isfahan, Iran

6. Besides the place it naturally occupies in every handbook of Islamic art, the "unifying" role of the geometric decor (analogous to the role of rhythm in architecture and music) has been specially studied by Issam el-Said and Ayse Parman in *Geometric Concepts in Islamic Arts* (London: World of Islam Festival Publishing, 1976) and by Keith Critchlow in *Islamic Patterns: An Analytical and Cosmological Approach* (London: Thames and Hudson, 1976).

The philosophical basis and the contemplative efficiency of geometric design and of the other components of Islamic art have been set out with remarkable clarity by Titus Burckhardt in *Art of Islam: Language and Meaning* (Bloomington, IN: World Wisdom, 2009); see in particular chap. IV dealing with "the common language of Islamic art".

The form of Arabic letters, their hieratic character—above all in the earliest transcriptions of the Koran—and the proportions which regulate all their outlines lead us to another mode of artistic expression to which the Arabs were certainly predisposed and for which Islam provided the occasion of an exceptional flowering. I have in mind the language of geometric figures and forms to which also is linked that of numbers.

By means of geometry, the Muslim artists have succeeded in illustrating visually a notion as sublime as that of *tajallī*, the infinite radiation of the Divine Essence across the multiplicity of levels of existence. The whole philosophy of arabesque and interlacement, whether it be floral or geometric, as of polygonal decoration, rests on the idea of an omnipresent center which manifests itself where and when it will without thereby being in any way, in its nature, affected, augmented, or diminished. The explosion of stars on the vault of a cupola—notably in the mosques of Persia, Turkey, and Central Asia—is an illustration of this thesis. As to the friezes of tracery which frame a door or a prayer niche, or which run under a ceiling, or which border a carpet, they are, like the march of time which regulates our lives, the reminder of the guiding thread which directs and coordinates all the worlds and all the beings and which is none other than the Divine Providence.[6]

Likewise, there is a conscious and deliberate analogy between the division of space which is effected by the networks of polygonal stars and the division of time which is at the base of psalmody as of Arabic poetry. Each polygonal network is constructed according to a geometric outline which starts with the division of the circle into equal parts. Depending on whether the circle is first divided into three, four, or five segments, the network has for its rhythmical base the equilateral triangle, the square, or the pentagon (the star of five points), as well as the multiples of these figures: the hexagon or two inverted triangles, the octagon or the star of eight points, etc. To all these figures and numbers are attached precise symbolic meanings, and correspondences with the planets and their revolutions, with the phenomena and cycles of nature, with colors, temperaments and humors, knowledge of which make up part of the traditional artistic teaching as is borne out by, among other writings, the letters of the Ikhwān al-Safā', written in the 4th century of the Hegira (10th century AD) which provide us with valuable information concerning the arts and sciences of the time.[7]

3—ART WITHIN THE CITY, OR HOW THE MESSAGE OF DIVINE UNITY BECOMES IMPRINTED IN THE MUSLIM LIVING ENVIRONMENT

❧ *A Sanctuary with Multiple Cells*

Seen from the sky or the surrounding hills, the Islamic city is easily recognizable by its appearance of a cellular conglomerate. "*Natura horret vacuum*", said the Ancients, and the Islamic city, which obeys the laws of nature, does not leave any vacant spaces. Dense and compact, it is

118. View of the city of Baghdad, Iraq
119. View of the city of Yazd, Iran

7. Cf. article *IKHWĀN AL-SAFĀ* in *E.I.(2)* by Yves Marquet and *infra*, part III, p.91.

criss-crossed with barely visible arteries: streets, and alleys which, rarely linear, may vanish under a group of houses and reappear only to sink once again into refreshing shade.

Each cell comprises a square or rectangular structure surrounding an inner courtyard onto which open living quarters of houses, or shops, workshops and storerooms of bazaars and caravanserais, or class and students' rooms of religious colleges—*madrasas*—or galleries and prayer halls of mosques. Even though the buildings may be of different sizes, the largest ones being used for religious or civil purposes and containing princely palaces with their courtyards and interior gardens, these quadrangular cells give the urban canvas a homogeneity akin to that of a biological organism, formed from similar and compatible elements, and able to multiply and interweave without undue interference as the city develops (figs. 129 & 130).

A city is, first of all, a site which is chosen according to certain criteria, some having a quasi-universal value: the presence of water, often drawn from a river flowing from neighboring mountains like the Barada in Damascus (fig. 120) or the Zayandeh Rud in Isfahan (fig. 121), and a strategic location at the crossing of important lines of communication. In all cases protection for the city must be guaranteed, whether it hoists itself up a rocky slope like the holy city of Moulay Idriss in the Zerhoun mountains of Morocco (fig. 127) and the many fortified villages of Yemen, of the Algerian Aures or Moroccan Atlas (fig. 128) or, if built on a plain, it surrounds itself with walls, towers, and fortified doors (figs. 123 & 124).

In fact every Muslim city is a *hurm*, a sacred place for its inhabitants, just as every mosque is a *hurm*

120. *Top left*: A plain city: Damascus and its *ghuta* (oasis). A network of irrigation canals carries water from the Barada river to the gardens which extend up to the edge of the desert; 121. *Top right*: The Khaju Bridge over the Zayandeh Rud river, Isfahan, Iran; 122. *Above center*: Ahuan caravanserai, Semnan, Iran; 123. *Center*: Bab Dakakine, Fez, Morocco: in the absence of natural defenses, the city surrounds itself with walls whose powerful gates were locked during the nigh; 124. *Bottom*: View of the inner city of Khiva, encircled by crenellated walls, Uzbekistan

and as every family house, folded in on itself, closed to the exterior and open to the courtyard, the garden, and the sky, is also a *hurm*, a sanctuary where the father officiates as an *imām* and the mother as unchallenged mistress of domestic life.

125. *Top left*: Aerial view of the Friday Mosque, Isfahan, Iran; **126.** *Top right*: Traditional architecture in the city of Sana'a, Yemen; **127.** *Center left*: A mountain city: Moulay Idriss Zerhoun, Morocco. A typical example of a sanctuary-city, it is the site of the mausoleum of Idriss I, a descendant of Prophet Muhammad, and founder of the first Moroccan kingdom (d. 792 AD); **128.** *Center right*: A *ksar* (fortified village) in the Draa Valley, south Morocco; **129.** *Bottom left*: Aerial view of a village in the Tafilalet, south Morocco: the compact structure of the Muslim city, composed of square or rectangular cells with a nucleus opening to the sky; **130.** *Bottom right*: Marrakesh, Morocco: invariably, a larger cell forms the focus around which smaller cells cluster; it is the mosque, which is the center of religious and community life

Above the horizontal plane of its terraced roofs, the Islamic city raises the vertical lines of its minarets (the tall towers attached to many mosques), from whose summit the Word of God, carried by the voices of the muezzins, unfolds upon the town, bathing it in the Message of Divine Unity.

When carrying out a detailed survey of sanctuaries located in the various quarters of the Fez medina, as part of a safeguarding programme sponsored by Unesco, the late Titus Burckhardt—who died in January 1984—noticed, after plotting on a map the sites from where the muezzins launched their appeals, that they covered the entire city area with a network of sound waves, transmitted around each minaret within a radius of 60 meters, which is the average range of the human voice. This meant that no citizen could be left oblivious of the time for prayer, the city having incorporated into its fabric a proportion linked with the function of "remembrance" (*dhikr*) which is the very *raison d'être* of the Message and, consequently, of all that is known as "Islamic art".

⮩ *The Religious Function: The Mosque*

The primary function of the Islamic city is, indeed, religious in nature, as illustrated by the fact that many urban cores have been formed around a sanctuary—like the Holy Ka'bah of Mecca or the tomb of Moulay Idriss I (fig. 127)—and that public life, trade and craftsmanship, places of learning, baths, are grouped around the great mosque, or Friday mosque, where the preaching *imām* and the faithful meet for the common prayer. A place for prayer, the mosque is also a center of teaching where learned members of the community, the *'ulamā'*, impart "in the path of God", i.e. without payment, the traditional sciences—Koranic exegesis, psalmody, *Hadīth*, Arabic linguistics, theology, law, and even mysticism (*tasawwuf*)—to an audience of students, among them craftsmen and tradesmen of the souk who, according to the advice of Prophet Muhammad, are "seeking knowledge from cradle to tomb". In addition, the mosque is a meeting place where it is not considered unbecoming to exchange news of a personal or community nature. Finally, it may be a place of asylum for fugitives, and every destitute is sure to receive within its precinct food, alms, and shelter.

> In houses which God has permitted to be raised and that His Name may be invoked in them,
> Therein praise Him at dawn and evening men whom neither trade nor sale deter from the remembrance of God, the performance of prayer, and the giving of alms.
>
> (Koran 24: 36-37)

131. Courtyard of the Prophet's Mosque, Medina, Saudi Arabia

132. *Mihrāb* of the Prophet's Mosque, Medina, Saudi Arabia

The first mosque of Islam was that built by the Prophet in Medina, adjoining his own house. It consisted of a courtyard onto which opened the quarters of his wives, and a covered portico whose roof was held up

133. *Left*: The Great Mosque of Dakar, Senegal, built in the 1960s by artisans from Morocco, testifies to the perenniality of the Arabo-Andalusian architectural tradition in its forms and spirit of sobriety. Its two ablution pavilions, like those of the Qarawiyyin Mosque in Fez, have their prototypes in the Courtyard of the Lions of the Alhambra Palace in Granada, Spain

134. *Center*: The *mihrāb* of the Great Mosque of Kairouan, Tunisia

135. *Bottom*: The *minbar* of the Sokullu Mosque in Istanbul, Turkey, built in 1571 by the great architect Sinān Pasha

by palm trunks. A spear stuck into the ground in front of the rear wall showed the direction of Mecca and a small wooden rostrum allowed the Prophet to be seen and heard by all when he addressed the audience.

Such are up to this day, together with the minaret which appeared in Fustāt (Cairo) and then in Medina after the Prophet's death, the main constituents of the mosque. Most of the time, the prayer hall is preceded, according to the original design of the Prophet in Medina, by a courtyard which is also used for prayer on crowded days (figs. 131 & 133) and which is generally fitted with basins and fountains for ablutions (figs. 46-50 & 52-53). In the prayer hall, the orientation toward the Ka'bah of Mecca is indicated by the *mihrāb* (figs. 132, 134 & 155), a recess in the form of a niche before which the *imām* stands when leading the prayer. Just before he preaches, the *imām* climbs a few steps up the *minbar*, the rostrum placed on the right of the *mihrāb*, taking care not to reach the platform situated at the top of the stairs and surmounted by a canopy, a place of eminence that only the Prophet, God's elect, was worthy of occupying (fig. 135).

↝ The Other Functions of the City

Around the mosque, as if the intention was to recall that they derive from and are subordinate to it, other buildings invariably constructed on a square or rectangular pattern fulfill their respective functions: didactic establishments ranging from the university (some cities like Cairo, Kairouan, and Fez (figs. 5 & 84) were the seat of renowned universities several centuries in advance of Europe) to the theological college, *madrasa*, found in any important township (figs. 78-84 & 136) and the modest Koranic school present in each quarter of the city (figs. 85-87); mausoleums housing the remains of princes and saintly persons

136. *Top*: Mosque-Madrasa of Registan square, Samarkand, Uzbekistan;
137. *Bottom left*: The Taj Mahal, Agra, India; **138**. *Bottom right*: Mausoleum of Farīd ad-Dīn ʿAttar, Neishabour, Iran

(figs. 137-138 & 143); commercial and handicraft compounds, covered bazaars, *qissariyas* selling jewels and precious materials, caravanserais serving as rest-houses for travelers, stores for their goods and meeting places for business transactions (figs. 107, 122 & 139-140).

139. *Left*: The Hatters market (Tcharsouk), Samarkand, Uzbekistan

140. *Right*: One of the alleys of the bazaar of Isfahan, Iran

141. *Left*: Stucco claustras of a house in Sana'a, Yemen; **142**. *Right*: Wooden balconies in an old street of Mecca, Saudi Arabia

143. *Top*: Tomb of Shaykh Niʻmatullāh, Mahan, Iran; **144**. *Center*:
Detail from the hospital and mausoleum of Keykavus I, Sivas,
Turkey; **145**. *Bottom*: Tiled inscription on the dome of the Shaykh
Lotfollah Mosque, Isfahan, Iran

As soon as one leaves the bustle of public spaces to enter the residential quarters, streets become narrower, walls barer, being pierced only with solid nailed doors and, higher up, a few openings often fitted with *mashrabiya*, or grids made of turned wood and behind which earthenware jars filled with drinking water used to be kept for cooling, and from which it is possible to observe without being seen, as through a judas hole, any person arriving (fig. 142). This is the domain of group and family privacy, where a stranger is not supposed to enter without a specific purpose or permission, being conscious in any case of treading in a reserved zone.

❧ *The Divine Mark of Calligraphy*

Read: in the Name of thy Lord the Most
    Bountiful
Who teaches by the pen,
Teaches man that which he knew not.
          (Koran 96: 3-5)

Just as the divine Word proclaimed from minarets is diffused in all directions, weaving a sound network in space, so is the written form present everywhere: on the pages of the billions of handwritten and printed Korans (figs. 151-154), copies of which are found in every Muslim home, on the epigraphic friezes of monuments (figs. 89, 90 & 103), and on a multitude of objects having a ritual purpose: candlesticks, lamps (fig. 160), lecterns, votive banners, embroidered cloths intended to be hung as a *mihrāb* or as a cover for a catafalque on the example of the black velvet *kiswah* which is wrapped each year around the Kaʻbah of Mecca (figs. 102 & 146). Weapons, jewels, and many domestic utensils also bear formulas quoted or derived from the Koran which have the virtue of keeping pernicious influences at bay and attracting divine protection to those who bear or use them, as well as to those who merely look at them. This is because the Word of God possesses a power of recollection that acts upon the best part of man, assembles his scattered energies, and concentrates them, "in the path of God", thereby giving him the best chances for spiritual enlightenment, since God has promised "the good end to those who revere Him" (Koran 7: 128).

The most constant object of this recollection is none

other than the Supreme Name of the Divine: *Allāh*, the Arabic word for God, which is to be seen inlaid in "square Kufic" characters on the facade of many a monument in Iran and Central Asia (figs. 143 & 149), traced in ornamental style—the so-called Thuluth—on the majolica coverings of Near and Middle Eastern sanctuaries and palaces, and written in various styles of calligraphy to recall the Message of *tawhīd* (Unity), wherever the human eye can perceive it with profit: not only in oratories but also in the merchant's boutique, the craftsman's workshop, and the family sitting room. Being the support of the Revelation, Arab letters are fundamentally sacred, and any word written in Arabic may have a connotation with some verse of the Holy Koran. This explains

146. *Top right*: Embroidered cloth covering the door to the Ka'bah; 147. *Center left*: Tiled inscription from the Tuman Akha Mosque, Samarkand, Uzbekistan; 148. *Center top*: Panel with carved inscription, Egypt; 149. *Center bottom*: Kufic calligraphy, Herat, Afghanistan; 150. *Center right*: Contemporary plate from Kutahya, Turkey; 151. *Bottom left*: Page from a North-African Koran in Maghrebi script, 1304; 152. *Bottom right*: Page from an Eastern Kufic Koran, Iraq, Persia, or Afghanistan, 1092

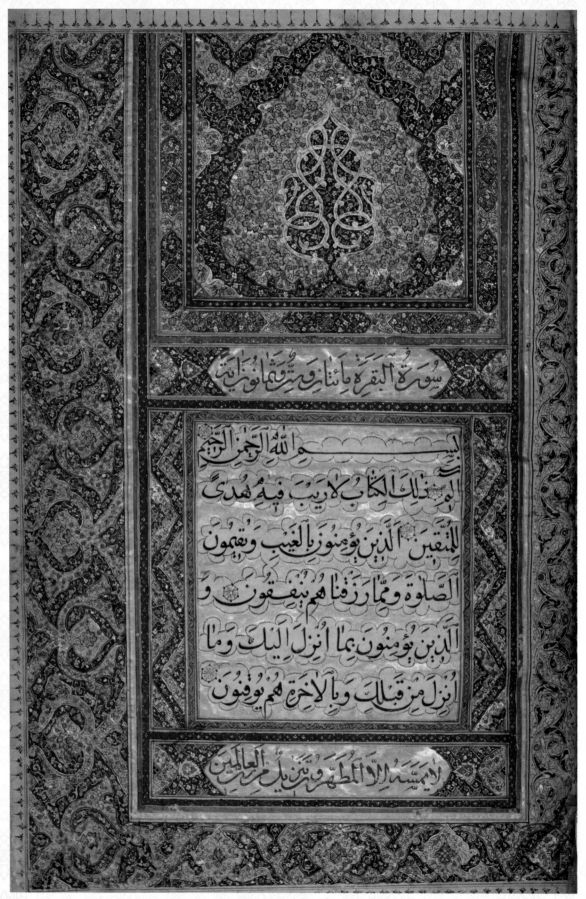

153. Ornamental page from a Persian Koran, 19th century

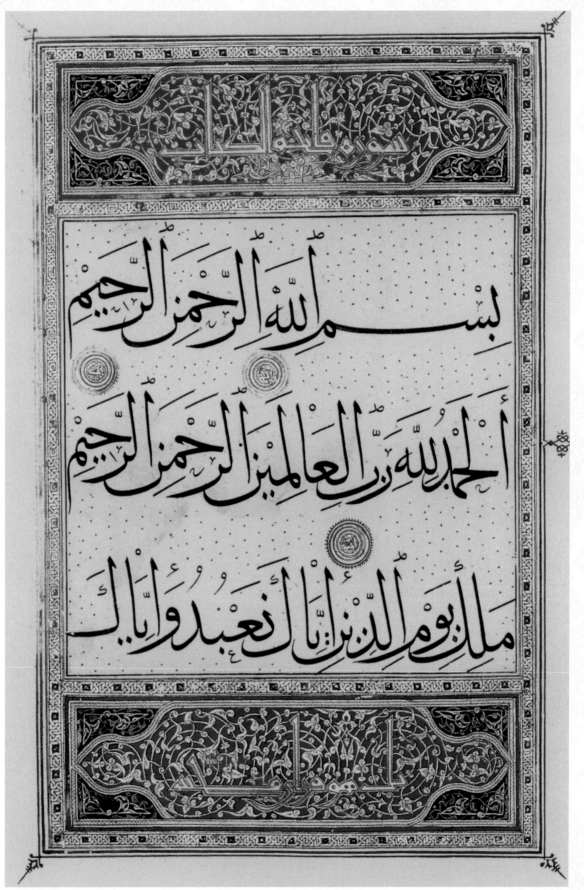

154. Opening chapter of the Koran, *Sūrat al-Fātihah*; Koran in Muhaqqaq script with *sūrah* headings in ornamental Kufic script, Cairo, Egypt, 1320-1330

155. Tiled *mihrāb* of the Madrasa Imami, Isfahan, Iran

why everyday utensils, like earthenware plates and bowls, copper trays and basins, which may come into contact with unclean substances, will only bear decorative pseudo-scripts without any meaning. Such is not the case, however, of an object like the plate shown in fig. 150 which bears in its center the apotropaic formula *mā shā' Allāh*, "what God wants", and will be laid upon a shelf or hung on the wall to remind the onlooker that nothing may happen, no material richness nor food may be obtained, if not through a divine Decree.

✧ Infinite Radiation and Omnipresent Center

The same spirit which presides over the calligraphic transcription of the Koranic Message and its recitation "embellished" by psalmody, giving form to a divinely inspired combination of horizontality and verticality, of melody and rhythm, is also found in the use of geometric decoration, whether applied to the art of illumination (figs. 96-97, 115 & 152-154) or to architecture (figs. 116-117, 155-157 & 163-164).

This type of decoration may assume one of two modes of expression which, in fact, are frequently associated: purely geometric patterns, built from regular polygons, and vegetal entrelacs, whose ramifications may include highly stylized and more or less fantasmagoric animal representations.

Both modes of expression obey the same laws of symmetry—with one or several axes—, of deployment starting from a point which itself is invisible in the final drawing. This point is the center of the circle which, divided into equal parts, serves to trace one or more figures radiating from it and filling the space attributed to them. In the case of vegetal designs representing either a tree with its branching twigs, leaves, and fruit, or a vase holding a bunch of flowers, the underlying geometric pattern confers on the picture a stability and firmness which, complemented by the flexibility of the stems that unfold, rise up, and fall down as does a fountain gushing in a basin, provide a fitting illustration of the harmonious coupling between essence and substance, heaven and earth, spirit and soul (fig. 156).

To evoke an omnipresent center, an indefinite and flawless creation because, as the Koran says, "You can see no fault in the All-Merciful's creation" (67: 3), such is the general meaning of the arabesque and entrelacs. Going further, according to the basic division which has been adopted, the compositions convey more precise symbolic meanings which are those of the cosmic threefold compound: Heaven, earth, and "what is between them", spirit, soul, and body; of the fourfold compound of stability and achievement; of the pentagram of the "Perfect Man"; of the hexagon—the "Seal of Solomon"—which unites in inverted directions the world of archetypes and their earthly reflections; of the sevenfold compound of the universal manifestation—"the seven heavens and seven earths" alluded to in the Koran; or of the octagon

156. *Top*: Floral decoration built on a geometric network, Registan, Sher Dor Madrasa, Samarkand, Uzbekistan

157. *Center*: *Zellij* from the Bahia Palace, Marrakesh, Morocco

158. *Bottom*: Around the courtyard of the al-'Attarin Madrasa in Fez, Morocco, claustras are made of an assembly of carved strips and elements of turned wood

159. *Top*: Ceramic panel *miḥrāb* reproducing *sūrah* 97, Kashan, Iran, 13th century

160. *Center*: Mosque lamp from Egypt, bearing the inscription of the "Verse of Light"

161. *Bottom*: Prayer rug with a niche design

belonging to the intermediary world, the plane of subtle entities, of creative Imagination which at the same time separates and links the Heaven and the earth just as, in architecture, the eight-faced drum serves as a transition between the square basis of a building and the dome which covers it (figs. 157-158).

As he works with numbers and parts of his body—the thumb, the opened hand, the elbow which provide him with standards— the Muslim artist reinterprets the universe as did the Pythagoreans, recreating and epitomizing it through the archetypical virtue of numbers and proportions.

❧ *God is Light*

Allāh is the Light of the heavens and the earth. The similitude of His light is as a niche wherein is a lamp. The lamp is in a glass. The glass is as it were a shining star, kindled from a blessed tree, an olive neither of the East nor of the West....

(Koran 24: 35)

Being one in its very nature and diverse in its manifestation, the light which shines on us is the most adequate symbol of the Divine and, among all the portents present in the created world, is for men the most conducive to the Source of all good.

The "Verse of Light" is one whose symbolic imagery has never ceased to feed the imagination of Muslim artists. This verse alone, over and above any reference to historic "loans", explains why the niche, in the form of the *miḥrāb*, has been adopted to indicate the direction of Mecca and mark the locus of the mosque. A lamp is often hung in front of the *miḥrāb*, reinforcing the importance of this architectural element as a support for concentration, in accordance with the literal meaning of the Verse of Light (fig. 160). As concerns the text of this verse, it is at times inscribed on mosque lamps, the finest of which were produced during the Mamluk period in Syrian and Egyptian workshops (fig. 160). The motif of the *miḥrāb*, whether or not accompanied by that of the lamp, has reached beyond the domain of architecture to imprint itself on many artifacts of metal, wood, or ceramics and, particularly, on carpets and wall hangings (figs. 161 & 191).

The dome, with which traditional architects cover their sanctuaries because it is an image of Heaven, serves as a mirror to capture and send down to the earth the "light of the heavens". This is the reason why it is sometimes covered with gold—like the Dome of the Rock in Jerusalem (fig. 162)—, with masonry ribs and interlacings—like the tombs of the Mamluk Sultans in Cairo (fig. 163)—, or with an enameled brick lining of bright turquoise, like the Timurid and Safavid monuments of Central Asia and Iran (figs. 138 & 164).

The whiteness, a symbol of the perfect Light, has to be tempered, shaded, colored, and diversified so as to be agreeable to the human eye

162. *Top left*: The Dome of the Rock, Jerusalem, Palestine; **163**. *Top center*: Qaytbay Mausoleum, Cairo, Egypt; *Top right*: **164**. *Top right*: Gur-e Amir Mausoleum, Samarkand, Uzbekistan; **165**. *Bottom*: Ceiling of the Shah Mosque, Isfahan, Iran

166. Stalactites from the decorative *muqarnas* at the pavilion of the Court of Lions, Alhambra, Granada, Spain

167. Arches with stucco decoration at the pavilion of the Court of Lions, Alhambra, Granada, Spain

168-169. *Top*: Carved plaster panels (left) and brick *muqarnas* (right) of the Abbasid Palace, Baghdad, Iraq

170. *Bottom left*: Lattice at the Taj Mahal, Agra, India; **171**. *Bottom right*: Mausoleum of Akbar, Sikandra, India

and, if not actually known—since the theologians maintain that the divine Essence is unknowable—at least sensed in its profound nature.

As with the irradiation (*tajallī*) of God into the creation, sunlight produces indefinite refractions on the various surfaces of the physical world. To grasp the order and harmony underlying this existential display, it is necessary for these refraction surfaces to be laid according to precise laws, the very laws that presided over the work of the supreme Artisan. Such is the fundamental meaning of the arabesques sculpted in plaster (figs. 167-168) and of the *muqarnas*, "stalactites" hanging from the ceiling of a vault, or the pendentives of a cupola (figs. 167 & 169). Being linked with sacred geometry, these architectural and/or decorative forms constitute what Titus Burckhardt has so ably described as an "alchemy of light", through which "the Muslim artist seeks to transform the very stuff he is fashioning into a vibration of light" (see p. 58 note 6).

In the realm of art, like in other branches of human activity, Islam does not set up a rigid partition between what relates to the highest aspirations of man and what responds to his biological and social needs. Not only, as we have seen earlier, does Islam not know of "art for the sake of art", but it instills in its artisans an ability to shape objects which at once are wholly adequate to serve a concrete purpose and conform to the art's own "unitarian" aesthetics.

For example, the characteristic element of Islamic architecture and furniture already referred to, i.e. the *mashrabiya*s—grid, grille, or lattice work—used to form many types of claustras and window screens fulfils an array of purposes of different orders: material, because a claustra offers protection against excessive sunlight and against possible intrusions, while allowing the air to circulate freely and bringing pleasant coolness inside the house; social, since it draws a limit between two spaces, external and internal, public and private, masculine and feminine or, in the case of ancient mosques, between the enclosure where the ruler used to sit and the general space allocated to the community; and, finally, aesthetic and spiritual because the lattice work through which the daylight penetrates into the indoor space confers on it a peculiar aura, a combination of order and harmony originating from the material and the geometric pattern chosen by the artisan to construct his grid.

Whether the claustra of a Moroccan *madrasa*, a sturdy network of turned-wood octagons (fig. 158), or the delicate netting of carved stone and marble in Mughal shrines and palaces (figs. 170-171), the effect on the soul is similar; it is of the same nature as the indefinite interplay of light and shadow, the cutting of space into crystalline fractions produced by arabesques and *muqarnas* sculpted in plaster, stone, or wood. In all these cases, it is the leitmotiv of the Unity of Being which can be perceived through the multiplicity of created forms.

172. *Top*: Berber wooden grid in a kasbah (fortress) in Agdz, Morocco

173. *Bottom*: Wooden lattice in al-Hakim Mosque, Isfahan, Iran

❧ Water as the Source of Life

We made of water every living thing (Koran 21: 30).

Allāh has created from water every living being.
(Koran 24: 45)

When the Divine Essence, unseizable in its own nature, aspires to be perceived, it overflows and reveals itself in a creative irradiation, as expressed in the sacred utterance (*hadīth qudsī*) inspired to Prophet Muhammad: "I was a hidden Treasure; then I desired to be known and created the creatures." At first, it condenses into an ethereal substance, the principle of the four cosmic elements which is sometimes called "the dust" or the "thick cloud". At times also, like in the biblical Genesis, it is designated as "the higher waters" or "the surface of waters" or simply, as in the above quoted Koranic verses, as "water". In this primordial sense, water is the *materia prima* which the Spirit comes to inform; it is the support of universal life.

The earthly water, a gift of God indispensable to the material and spiritual life of every human being, is a common property, and every ruler or group leader has the obligation to ensure its equitable distribution to all members of the community. This explains the remarkable degree of development achieved in all Muslim countries with hydraulic works that are found in the countryside and city alike: irrigation canals and pools, water wheels and aqueducts (figs. 176-177), public fountains (fig. 52), not to mention the facilities needed for the ritual purification in the form of baths, latrines, and ablution basins (figs. 46-53).

Water is joy, plenitude and, in the garden, it flows and sings permanently. When it is not physically present, because of unfavorable climatic or housing conditions, an effort is made to at least suggest its presence by some symbolic means: the cruciform design of the alleys and pavement of the inner courtyard of a house, recalling the four rivers flowing in Paradise, or the orderly placing of plant and flower

174. *Top*: A courtyard of a house in Córdoba, Spain

175. *Bottom*: The fountain of the Court of Lions, Alhambra, Granada, Spain

176. Irrigation at Kerzaz, Algeria; **177**. Water wheel on the Orontes river, Hama, Syria

178. *Above left:* The Fin Gardens, Kashan, Iran; **179**. *Above right*: The Generalife Gardens, Alhambra, Granada, Spain

180. *Bottom*: The Bagh-e Faiz Baksh, Shalimar Gardens, Lahore, Pakistan pots to draw the outline of a *ryad*, the classical closed garden with its partitioned borders and beds of vegetation.

In Arabic, the same word *jannah*, often appearing in the Koran, may be used to designate either the earthly or the heavenly garden and, for a Muslim, any garden, whether richly arranged or modest, must allow the imagination a precursory sense of the joys that await the elect in their happy abode. Among the elements which help to enhance this relationship, a few have been particularly cherished by the master gardeners of Islam: the inverted image of earthly things and the reflection of the sky appearing on the surface of a basin (fig. 179); the actual or figurative presence of the four rivers of Eden (fig. 175); the planting of trees endowed with eternal youth, like yews and cypresses, or bearing the fruits of Paradise, like dates and pomegranates mentioned in the Koranic descriptions of the heavenly Garden; the selection of flowers whose fragrance is suggestive of an immaterial beatitude; and the setting up of "dwellings" analogous to those reserved for the companions of Heaven, in the form of tents woven with many-colored brocades, of pergolas and pavilions placed at strategic points

181. *Left*: *Rustam with His Mistress in a Garden Pavilion*, Mughal miniature, 15th century

182. *Right*: Mughal miniature showing the garden of Bagh-e Vafa, near Kabul, Afghanistan, 1508

183. *Center*: The Generalife Gardens, Alhambra, Granada, Spain

184. *Bottom right*: Palais Jamai, Fez, Morocco

from where the view offers a perspective of lanes, rivulets, and plots (figs. 183-184). Finally, various devices help to associate hearing with the other senses in this place of delight when landscape architects cause water to zigzag then fall back into marble basins, so that the murmur of the stream mixes with the cooing of doves.

❧ *Representational Art is not Excluded*

Following in the tracks of Abraham, the *hanīf*, "pure" servant of the One God, who would certainly have disapproved the placing of hundreds of anthropomorphic statues in and around the Ka'bah erected with his own hands, Prophet Muhammad when victoriously entering Mecca on completion of his mission struck down with his stick all these idols while crying out: "Truth has come and falsehood has vanished!" (Koran 17: 81). This gesture has henceforth served as an example, so that no human figuration has ever appeared in a religious monument of Islam.

In other respects, judging by the sculptures and engravings which have reached us from pre-Islamic Arabia and Yemen, it does not seem as if the inhabitants of these regions, the very people who were to become the first Muslims, were particularly gifted for representational

185. *Horsemen Waiting to Participate in a Parade*; from the *Maqāmāt of al-Harīrī*, Baghdad, Iraq, 13th century

186. *Youth Reading*, Deccani School, India, c. 1610; **187**. *Mughal miniature, 18th century*

work. As for what is known of the early Arab painting, which served to decorate with frescoes the Umayyad palaces of the Syrian desert and, later, the first illustrated scientific manuscripts, it is so closely inspired by its previous models—Hellenistic, Mesopotamian, and Persian—that it can hardly be called "Islamic".

In fact, in the case of representational painting, unlike the other forms of art—architecture, geometric decor, calligraphy, and, as we shall see, music—, it took a long time for Islam to assimilate the existing traditions and develop an individual style. For almost six centuries, it was content to adopt "foreign" themes and prototypes slightly altering them to suit its own purposes. It is only from the 13th century onward that one can speak of a typically Islamic style of representational illustration which, applied to the art of the book and associated with calligraphy and floral or geometric illumination, has produced countless masterworks in several parts of the Islamic world.

A first branch of this art with a strong Arabic imprint has blossomed in the Near East, in Syria, Iraq (fig. 185), and Egypt; another developed in areas under a Turkish influence, itself impregnated with Chinese culture; and a third, the richest and liveliest, was nurtured by Iran which raised it to unique heights of beauty and technical achievement.

188. *Left*: Safavid miniature, 16th century

189. *Right*: *The Prophet and the Angel*, Safavid miniature, 16th century

Persian painting, even though it is miniaturized to fit the format of a book, thus allowing it to escape the censure of literalist mullahs, possesses an obvious spiritual dimension. It incites to meditation, either directly when illustrating religious subjects (fig. 189), or indirectly when representing allegoric gardens and landscapes, mythico-historic episodes, and familiar scenes where persons are drawn hieratically and fitted into vertical compositions which converge toward the sky or the domes of delicately adorned pavilions (fig. 188).

In Mughal India, another synthesis took place under the aegis of Islam between the Persian and Indian schools of painting, giving birth to a style where handsome princes and noble persons are portrayed holding a rose or their favorite falcon and enjoying the harmony that surrounds them, whether taken up with the pleasures of hunting and love or absorbed in pious meditation (figs. 186-187).

❧   *Simple Life*

O men, you are the poor toward God. He, God, is the Rich, the infinitely Praised! (Koran 35: 15)

Even after the Muslim community had organized itself into cities, it retained a perpetual nostalgia for the nomadic life and, even during its most refined periods, did not abandon some of the habits of simplicity inherited from the desert. From Baghdad to Fez, through Damascus and Cairo, the "Arabs"—a term used to designate, with a certain

190. *Top*: Floor carpet detail, Uzbekistan; **191**. *Center*: Bokhara *ensi* carpet;
192. *Bottom*: Tent and loom of the Bedouin Bani Na'imāt, south Jordan

193. *Top*: Folk Festival in the Berber Zemmour tribe (Khemisset Province), Morocco

194. *Center left*: So-called "Kuwaiti chest" produced in the Gulf area: Iraq, Bahrain, Oman; made of wood (*tamr hindi*) imported from India and decorated with brass hinges, plates, and nails

195. *Bottom left*: Painted chest of the Jbaala country, in the vicinity of Tangiers, Morocco. The arcade motif shows how the urban Hispano-Moresque style of decoration has found its way to the very heart of rural areas

196. *Bottom right*: Carpet from Moroccan High Atlas area

esteem, the itinerant Bedouins, the "men of the tent"—have acquired a reputation for the purity of their mores, their generosity, their sense of honor, and the quality of their eloquence and language, to such an extent that until quite recently the great urban families of Syria and Iraq used to arrange for their sons to spend long periods with their desert cousins before engaging in professional and family life.

In the richest as well as the poorest Muslim houses, furniture and household utensils lend themselves to polyvalent use of space, in the same way as in a Bedouin tent. Guests—as many as can be

accommodated—are seated on cushions placed along the walls, are served meals around large trays brought in at the time of eating and taken away immediately afterward and, when night comes, are invited to lie on carpets and wrap themselves in blankets which up till then were piled in a corner of the room.

Rather than furniture, the principal item of which is the chest (figs. 194-195), used as a cupboard or as a trunk, it is the carpet which "furnishes" the domestic space, confers on it a quasi-sacred character, making it a privileged place (*harīm*) in which the privacy of the family group is tightened and where the individual seated on the carpet feels invited to recollect and meditate. A cosmos in reduction, the carpet seeks to evoke, through its centralized composition, the place which is allotted to man as viceregent within the creation (fig. 196). On a prayer carpet, the presence of a *mihrāb* (fig. 191), a lamp, a pair of candlesticks, aids concentration during the rite. In other cases, the place represented is the dwelling of primordial man, the Garden of Eden crossed by four rivers: one of inalterable milk, one of pure honey, one of a wine that does not inebriate, and one of a water which never stagnates (Koran, *passim* and 47: 15), where birds sing, gazelles leap, roses, jasmines, and tulips blossom and never fade away.

❧ *The God-loved Artisan*

God loves the believing servant who practices a craft. (*Hadīth*)

It would be unfair to describe the imprint conferred by art on the Muslim world without mentioning those who, in the anonymity and inconspicuousness that characterize the "poor toward God", have played the main part in shaping this universe with their own hands. These artisans, whose welcoming workshops are often open late at night

197. Basket weaver, Salalah, Oman
198. Coppersmith shop, bazaar in Isfahan, Iran
199. Silversmith, Buramy, Oman
200. Traditional embroidery, Morocco

everywhere from the Far-East to the Far-West of the Muslim world, are typically humble and honest, intelligent and pious, conscious of the values of which they are the depositaries and which they endeavor to keep alive, often in unrewarding circumstances.

Let us refer once again to the saying of Prophet Muhammad: "God loves that when one of you does something he does it thoroughly". *Itqān*, thoroughness, the search for perfection—even though every artisan knows that true Perfection belongs only to God—goes hand in hand with *ihsān*, virtuous behavior, which is indicative of a certain degree of nearness to God.

The close links existing between the practice of handicrafts and a life conducted on "the Right Path"—*al-sirāt al-mustaqīm* often mentioned in the Koran—are also founded in the knowledge, according to ancient

201. Coppersmith in Isfahan, Iran

202. Weavers in Morocco

203. Silversmith in Isfahan, Iran

204. A potter in Morocco

205. Weaver in the village of Harrania, close to the Pyramids, Egypt

206. Embroidery workshop, Rabat, Morocco

207. Potter in the Coptic neighborhood of
Cairo, Egypt

208. Qashqais carpet weaver, Iran

8. Cf. M. Lings, *A Sufi Saint of the Twentieth Century, Shaykh Ahmad al 'Alawī*, 3rd
ed. (Louisville, Kentucky: The Islamic
Texts Society, 1993).

9. Cf. article *HĀSHIMĪ* in *E.I.* (2) by J.-L.
Michon.

traditions, that most crafts were initially taught to men by the prophets. The art of weaving, for instance, goes back to Shīth (Seth), a son of Adam; carpentry originates from Seyidnā Nūh (Noah), to whom God revealed the way of building the Ark, etc. The memory of these saintly teachers was kept alive in the initiation ceremonies and other rituals which were performed until a very recent time by the craft guilds and brotherhoods of Islam.

Many great scholars of religious science and masters of the mystical path originated from the world of craftsmanship. Such was the case, during our century, of Shaykh Ahmad al-'Alawī from Mostaghanem, Algeria, who died in 1934. A cobbler by profession, he attained such sanctity that thousands of disciples were attracted to his *zawiya*, coming from all parts of the Islamic world, and even Europe.[8] He designated as his lieutenant in the Near East Muhammad al-Hāshimī al-Tilimsānī, whose classes I had the good fortune to attend when living in Damascus, a city where he had migrated from Algeria in 1911, and where he died in 1961. He had been trained as a tailor, a craft which he practiced until his functions as *'ālim*, teaching Koranic law and theology in the Great Umayyad Mosque and Sufism in his own home, took up all his time. He, too, was a man of high spirituality and intense fervor in the performance of his duties toward God and men.[9]

EPILOGUE

Today, in all parts of the Muslim world, many craftsmen are abandoning their trades, for want of patronage, to become employees or workers in industry, or sometimes—if they are lucky—*shawush*, that is to say office boys in government administration; they do this only out of necessity, half-heartedly, because the ancestral crafts are no longer able to support them and their families.

In a world already so impoverished in spiritual values, where the West has long since lost its sacred art, can one stand by with indifference and watch the steady disappearance of an incomparable form of expression? "Incomparable" because the language of Islamic art is, I hope I have been able to show, of supra-human inspiration. It is the reflection, in material shaped by man, of spiritual truths, the *haqā'iq*, of which man has received the imprint. Making these truths perceptible, the artist leaves testimonies of the Divine Solicitude exercised with regard to our world.

The whole of Islamic art, in its prestigious monuments as in its more modest creations, bears testimony to the truth of the Message received fourteen centuries ago by the Prophet Muhammad. It also demonstrates the efficacy and vitality of the Message across time and space. Finally, by its persuasive beauty, it attracts those who come into contact with it.

Tamerlane the Destroyer (1336-1405), who without the least pity was able to massacre the inhabitants of entire cities, nevertheless spared the guardians of religious science—*'ulamā'* and *fuqahā'*—and also artists whom he carried away to embellish his capital, Samarkand.

Are we to conclude that modern states, in their pursuit of technological power and economic profit, will be shown to be more destructive of traditional values than the armies of Tamerlane? One would like to answer negatively, particularly as it is wrong to assume that the improvement of living conditions necessarily entails the sacrifice of traditional craftsmen.

Certain Muslim community leaders are still aware of the role that authentic art should continue to play in the Islamic city. Much has been said in recent years about safeguarding and rehabilitating the old Islamic cities, the medinas, and about the conservation of living handicrafts.[10] In fact, this is not only a problem for Muslims; it has to do with the concern for maintenance or restoration of the quality of life everywhere in the world. Thus the attention of many Western architects, town planners, and social scientists is drawn to the Arabo-Islamic model which they use as a reference when looking for solutions to create "a better world", where there would be a balance between technological constraints and human needs and aspirations.

There is today in the Muslim world a new generation of architects, planners, and human science specialists who are worried by and react against the destruction, due to neglect or speculation, of valuable natural and cultural assets. May their protests and common endeavors lead to carefully planned and implemented policies for conservation and promotion of the national heritage, so that by the fruits which are the works of art we may continue to know the blessed Tree which produced them and brought them to maturity.[11]

10. Among the many international meetings on the Islamic city which have been held during the last decades one may quote the following, the proceedings of which have been published:

—ICOMOS, Second Conference on the Conservation, Restoration, and Revival of Areas and Groups of Buildings of Historic Interest, Tunis, June 1968.

—Middle East Center, Cambridge, U.K./Unesco, Colloquium on the Islamic City, July 1976 (see p. 4, note 1).

—The Aga Khan Award for Architecture, Seminar Two in the series "Architectural Transformations in the Islamic World", *Conservation as Cultural Survival*, Istanbul, September 1978.

—Organization of Arab Cities/Government of Saudi Arabia, Symposium on the Arab City, Madinah Munawwarah, 2 Feb.-5 March 1981.

Under the World Heritage Convention established by Unesco, a number of historic cities of the Muslim world have been included in the World Heritage List. They are (by alphabetical order, up to 1992): Aleppo, Cairo, Damascus, Djenné (Mali), Fez, Isfahan, Istanbul, Jerusalem, Marrakesh, Kairouan, Sana'a, Timbuktu, and Tunis.

11. As regards craftsmanship, recent developments indicate that safeguard and promotion of traditional arts and crafts are now receiving attention from many governments, including Members of the Organization of the Islamic Conference. An International Seminar on Prospects of Development of Traditional Crafts in OIC countries has been held in Rabat in October 1991 and its proceedings published by the Research Center for Islamic History, Art, and Culture (IRCICA) in Istanbul. As a follow up of that meeting, a First International Islamic Artisans at Work Festival has taken place in Islamabad from 7 to 15 October 1994. Two thousand craftsmen from thirty countries have been able to demonstrate their crafts and eighty awards have been distributed. In connection with the Festival, a joint Unesco/IRCICA/Lok Virsa Seminar on Creativity in Traditional Islamic Crafts has reviewed the problems encountered by craftsmen to adapt to new needs and expectations, and a number of recommendations have been put forward.

PART III

MUSIC AND SPIRITUALITY IN ISLAM

PART III

MUSIC AND SPIRITUALITY IN ISLAM

1—A CONTROVERSIAL QUESTION

"Oh Lord! Make us to see things as they are!" asked the Prophet Muhammad when addressing himself to his Lord.[1] The same prayer was to be repeated later over and over by devout Muslims desiring to objectively judge a more or less ambiguous situation. It is therefore well-placed at the beginning of an essay on the art of music such as it was and such as it is still practiced in the countries of the *dār al-Islām* and by the people who comprise it. Few subjects have been debated or have raised as many contradictory emotions and opinions as the status of music *vis-à-vis* religious Law and at the heart of Muslim society. In fact the debate is not yet over and, no doubt, never will be because it concerns a domain in which it seems that Providence wanted to give Muslims the greatest possible freedom of choice and of appreciation. No Koranic prescription explicitly aims at music; the *Sunnah*, the "customs" of the Prophet, cites only anecdotal elements, none of which constitutes a peremptory argument either for or against musical practice; and the third source of Islamic Law, the opinion of doctors of the Law, spokesmen recognized by social consensus, varies extremely, ranging from a categorical condemnation of music to its panegyric while passing through various degrees of acceptance and reservation.

To understand how such divergent positions could have arisen and been expressed on this subject in the same context of Islamic thought and ethics, it is useful to refer to those interpreters who knew how to take into consideration ideas at once metaphysical, philosophical, or theosophical as well as the imperatives of the Muslim ethics, both individual and social. To this category belong the Ikhwān al-Safā', the "Brethren of Purity",* whose vast encyclopedia of philosophy, science, and art, compiled in the 4th/10th century, contains a precious "Epistle on Music".[2]

Like the Greek philosophers, the Ikhwān recognized in terrestrial music the echo of the music of the spheres, "inhabited by the angels of God and by the elite of his servants". Thus, "the rhythm produced by the motion of the musician evokes for certain souls residing in the world of generation and corruption the felicity of the world of the spheres, in the same way that the rhythms produced by the motion of the spheres and the stars evoke for souls who are there the beatitude of the world of the spirit." By reason of the law of harmony which reigns over all the planes of existence, linking them according to an order at once hierarchical and analogical, "the caused beings belonging to secondary reactions imitate in their modalities the first beings which are their causes ... from which it must be deduced that the notes of terrestrial music necessarily imitate those of celestial music". Like

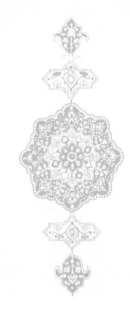

209. *Preceding page*: Carpet from Kerman, Iran

210. *Opposite*: *Joseph Listening to Music,* from the manuscript *Yusuf and Zulaykha* by Jāmī, Tabriz, Iran, 1540

1. *Arīnā' l-ashyā kamā hiya: hadīth* cited by Fakhr al-Dīn al-Rāzī in his "Great Commentary" on the Koran (*Mafātih al-ghayb*) with respect to the verse XVII, 85: "They will question thee concerning the Spirit....", *Al-Tafsīr al-kabīr*, 2nd ed. (Tehran, n.d.), vols. 21-22, p. 37. Also cited by Hujwīrī in his *Kashf al-mahjūb* (see note 5 below) with respect specifically to the contradictory opinions concerning the spiritual concert (*al-samā'*).

2. The complete work includes 51 (or 52) "Epistles" (*Rasā'il*) of which the one treating music is the fifth. See "L'épître sur la musique des Ikhwān al-safā'", translation annotated by A. Shiloah, *Revue des études islamiques* (*REI*), 31 (1964), 125-162; 33 (1966), 159-193. The passages cited hereafter are found on pages 155-158 (1964).

* Publisher's Note: The Ikhwān al-Safā' were an esoteric organization of Arab Muslim philosophers in Basrah, Iraq, the seat of the Abbasid Caliphate in the 10th century AD.

211. Drums, tambourines, and flutes

Pythagoras, who "heard, thanks to the purity of the substance of his soul and the wisdom of his heart, the music produced by the rotation of the spheres and the stars" and who "was the first to have spoken of this science", other philosophers such as Nichomacus, Ptolemy, and Euclid, had "the habit of singing, with percussive sounds produced by chords, words, and measured verses that were composed for exhortation to the spiritual life and described the delights of the world of the spirit, the pleasure and the happiness of its inhabitants". Thus later came the Muslim conquerors who, when given the signal to attack, recited certain verses of the Koran or declaimed Arabic or Persian poems describing the paradisal delights reserved for those who died while fighting on the path of God. When resorting to music, when inventing the principles of its melodies and the constitution of its rhythms, the sages had no other goal than "to soften hardened hearts, to wake the negligent souls from their sleep of forgetfulness and the misguided spirits from their slumber of ignorance, to make them desire their spiritual world, their luminous place and their journey of life, to make them leave the world of generation and corruption, to save them from submersion in the ocean of the material world and to deliver them from the prison of nature".

How, under these circumstances, can it be explained that music could become an object of reprobation? Because, explain the Ikhwān, even if it is good in itself, music can be turned aside from its natural and legitimate ends: "As for the reason for the interdiction of music in certain laws of the prophets … it relates to the fact that people do not use music for the purpose assigned it by the philosophers, but for the purpose of diversion, for sport, for the incitation to enjoy the pleasures of this lower world." Thus, that which can become reprehensible is not music itself but the use to which certain people put it. "Be watchful while listening to music, that the appetites of the animal soul do not push you toward the splendor of nature. Nature will lead you astray from the paths of salvation and prevent you from discourse with the superior soul."[3] This warning issued by the Ikhwān goes along with the teaching given a century earlier by the Sufi Dhū'l-Nun the Egyptian (d. 246/861): "Listening (*al-samā‘*) is a divine influence which stirs the heart to see *Allāh*; those who listen to it spiritually attain to *Allāh*, and those who listen to it sensually fall into heresy."[4] In the same way, Hujwīrī wrote in his *Kashf al-mahjūb* ("The Lifting of the Veil"), the first treatise on Sufism written in Persian,[5] "Listening to sweet sounds produces an effervescence of the substance molded in man; true, if the substance be true, false, if the substance be false".

Such was, generally speaking, the attitude of the philosophers and theoreticians of music, as well as that of the majority of Sufis and a good number of canonists. Aware of the benefits of the art of music, they did not show themselves less circumspect as to its utilization, distinguishing between noble and vulgar genres, between sensual melodies, "useful" melodies,[6] etc.

3. A. Shiloah, *REI* 33 (1966), 185. In the same way, F. Schuon writes, "while listening to beautiful music, the guilty will feel innocent. But the contemplative, on the contrary, while listening to the same music, will forget himself while fathoming the essences.…" (*Sur les traces de la religion pérenne* [Paris: Le Courier du Livre, 1982], 66-67).

4. Cited by H.G. Farmer, *A History of Arabian Music* (London, 1929; reprinted 1973), 36.

5. In the second half of the 5th/11th century, according to R.A. Nicholson who gave an English translation of it in the E.J.W. Gibb Memorial Series, vol. XVII (London: Luzac, 1911; repr. 1959).

6. As by Ibn ‘Alī al-Kātib who cites al-Fārābī. Cf. A. Shiloah, La Perfection des connaissances musicales (Paris: Geuthner, 1972), 65-68.

However, numerous jurists went much further and, seeing the evil usage which could be made of the practice of music, concluded that music itself was evil or, at least, that it involved more disadvantages than advantages and had, therefore, to be banned from society. Poetry which was sung and the use of instruments gave rise, they said, to corrupting excitations of the soul which turned the individual aside from his religious duties, encouraged him to seek out sensual satisfactions and bad company, pushed him into drunkenness and debauchery. Such jurists went so far as to say that the public singer, even if he sings the Koran to arouse pleasure in his listeners, could not be heard as a legal witness. They also maintained that it was lawful to break musical instruments.[7]

For the jurist and moralist Ibn Abī'l-Dunyā (d. 281/894), who wrote a short treatise on the "Censure of Instruments of Diversion" (*Dhamm al-mālāhī*),[8] singing and music were condemnable distractions of the same type as the games of chess and backgammon.

Later the Hanbalite jurist Ibn al-Jawzī (d. 597/1200) was to show himself to be just as severe *vis-à-vis* music which the evil human nature, "the soul which incites to evil", according to the Koran (12: 53) has a tendency to seize upon in order to anchor man in sensuality. "The spiritual concert (*al-samā‘*) includes two things", he wrote in his *Talbīs Iblīs* ("The Dissimulation of the Devil"). "In the first place, it leads the heart away from reflection upon the power of God and from assiduity in His service. In the second place, it encourages enjoyment of the pleasures of this world. . . ." And furthermore, "Music makes man forget moderation and it troubles his mind. This implies that man, when he is excited, commits things which he judges reprehensible in others when he is in his normal state. He makes movements with his head, claps his hands, strikes the ground with his feet, and commits acts similar to those of the insane. Music leads one to this; its action appears to be like that of wine, because it clouds the mind. This is why it is necessary to prohibit it."[9]

Ibn al-Jawzī admits however that there are certain musical genres in which the emotional element does not enter and which, therefore, are legal, such as songs of pilgrims to Mecca, songs of fighters for the faith, and songs of camel drivers. He recognized also that in a previous epoch in which Ibn Hanbal lived (3rd/9th century), poems were sung which exalted only religious feeling and which, consequently, escaped interdiction. But such times, according to him, are over and the innovations introduced since then in music and poetry are such that these arts can only have a deleterious influence.

2—THE PHILOSOPHER-MUSICOLOGISTS

Although they must be regarded as admissible on the part of the jurists who are concerned above all with the moral health of the common man

7. On this question see especially H.G. Farmer, *A History*, chap. II, "Islam and Music", J. Robson (cf. note 8 below) and M. Molé (cf. note 9 below).

8. A translation was made of this by J. Robson, *Tracts on Listening to Music*, Oriental Translation Fund, n.s., XXXIV, R.A.S. (London: Royal Asiatic Society, 1938). It is followed by the translation of the treatise entitled *Bawāriq al-ilmā‘* by the Sufi Ahmad al-Ghazzālī surnamed Majd al-Dīn (d. 520/1126), brother of the celebrated Abū Hāmid al-Ghazzālī (Algazel), author of the *Ihyā'*. In contrast to Ibn Abī'l-Dunyā, Ahmad Ghazzālī supports the legality of music and exalts the virtues of the spiritual concert. In his introduction to these two treatises (1-13), J. Robson summarizes well the arguments employed by the defenders of these antithetical positions.

9. Cited by M. Molé in *Les Danses sacrées*, "La Danse extatique en Islam" (Paris: le Seuil, 1963), 164. This study contains abundant documentation, drawn from original and often little known sources, on the arguments for and against the use of music and dance in the mystical path.

and the collectivity, arguments of this nature cannot be held as applying to those seekers of Truth who have sufficiently refined themselves so as not to fall into the trap of sensuality, for whom music occupies an important place in the hierarchy of the arts and the sciences and who consider and practice it as a discipline capable of elevating man above the gross world, of making him to participate in the universal harmony. Such seekers have been numerous from early times in the Islamic world which, thanks to them, can pride itself on an extremely fecund tradition on the level of theory as well as that of the practice of vocal and instrumental music.

Among the theoreticians who thought and wrote about music, two clearly distinguishable schools can be recognized which sometimes converged but, more often, went along their separate paths, drawing upon their own sources and applying different methods of investigation. They are, on one side, the philosophers (sages), and, on the other side, the mystics (Sufis).

To the first group are linked the great thinkers whose names are forever inseparable from the history of Islamic philosophy, names such as Yaʿqūb al-Kindī (d. appr. 252/866), Abū Bakr al-Rāzī (Rhazes, 311/923), Abū Naṣr al-Fārābī (338/950), whose "Great Book on Music" achieved considerable fame, Ibn Sīnā (Avicenna, 428/1037), Ibn Bājja (Avempace, d. 532/1138), and Ṣafī al-Dīn (629/1293).[10] If they all inherited the legacy of ancient Greece and resumed the Pythagorian, Aristotelian, Platonic, and Neoplatonic discourse, they imprinted upon it a unique and profoundly original mark, enriching it not only with numerous scientific developments but with the whole school of thought based on Koranic Revelation.[11] The Ikhwān al-Ṣafāʾ previously mentioned also belonged to this group. Their "Epistle on Music" opens as follows:

> After having completed the study of the theoretical spiritual arts which are of a scientific genre, and the study of the corporeal, practical arts which are the *genera* of the arts, . . . we propose in the present epistle entitled "Music" to study the art which is made up of both the corporeal and the spiritual. It is the art of harmony which can be defined by the function of proportions.[12]

Two ideas, therefore, impose themselves at the onset, the first being that music is composed of corporeal and spiritual elements, the second that it is based on proportions. Due to its dual composition the art of music possesses the special power of freeing matter in order to spiritualize it, and of materializing the spiritual in order to render it perceptible. This power comes also from the fact that music is a science of proportions, as the Ikhwān explain in another epistle (the sixth) in which, after having shown by examples how number, proportion, and numerical relationship are applied to all phenomena they add, "All these examples demonstrate the nobility of the science of proportion

212. Detail from a Persian miniature, late 16th century

10. On all these philosophers, who wrote extensively on musical theory, see under respective names *E.I.* (*1, 2*) and works of Baron R. d'Erlanger and H.G. Farmer.

11. For a better understanding of the Greco-Islamic affinities and their influence on musical science, one should consult the works of H.G. Farmer, especially: *The Sources of Arabian Music* (Glasgow: Glasgow Bibliographical Society, 1939 and Leyden: Brill, 1965) which includes the writings of Arabic authors. See also P. Kraus, *Jābir ibn Hayyān, contribution à l'histoire des idées scientifiques dans l'Islam: Jābir et la science grecque* (Paris: Les Belles Lettres, 1986), Y. Marquet, "Imamat, résurrection et hiérarchie selon les Ikhwān as-Safa" in *REI* 29 (1962), 49-142, E. Werner and J. Sonne, "The Philosophy and Theory of Music in Judeo-Arabic Literature", in *Hebrew Union College Annual*, XVI-XVII, wherein three chapters concerning the music are translated from the *Kitāb ādāb al-falāsifa* of Hunayn ibn Ishāq.

12. *REI* 31 (1964), 126-127 (see note 2 above).

which is music. This science is necessary for all the arts. Nevertheless, if it was connected with the name of music it is because music offers the best illustration of harmony".[13]

That which, according to the Ikhwān, characterizes music and distinguishes it from other arts is that the substance upon which it works, the soul of the listeners, like the elements which it employs, notes and rhythms, are of a subtle nature and not corporeal. "Music leaves in the souls of those who listen to it diverse impressions similar to those left by the work of the artisan in the matter which is the substratum of his art." And the Ikhwān cite many examples of emotional states which melodies are capable of inspiring in man, such as regret and repentance for past mistakes, courage in battle, relief from suffering, joyful excitation. Animals themselves are roused by hearing music, the camel quickens his step upon hearing the song of the camel-driver, the horse drinks more willingly when his master whistles a tune, the gazelle allows herself to be approached at night by the hunter who hums a melody.

"Music", exclaimed also Ibn Khurdādhbih (d. approx. 300/912), who was educated in Baghdad by the inspired Ishāq al-Mawsilī,[14] when introducing a speech delivered at the court of Caliph al-Mu'tamid, his protector and friend, "sharpens the intellect, softens the disposition, and agitates the soul. It gives cheer and courage to the heart, and high-mindedness to the debased.... It is to be preferred to speech, as health would be to sickness...."[15]

Not only does music stir the soul and the emotions, it "descends" into the body and from there comes its power to move the body and make it dance, and from there also come the therapeutic applications to which the classical treatises refer, notably those of al-Kindī and Ibn Sīnā. Besides this, it "rises" as far as the spirit because it is itself a vibration of supernatural origin like the *kun* ("Be!"), the primordial *fiat lux* from which, from nothingness, from silence, from darkness, existence was brought forth. Thus the remark of Ibn Zaylah (d. 440/1048), disciple of Ibn Sīnā, "Sound produces an influence on the soul in two directions. One is on account of its special composition, i.e. its physical content, the other on account of its being similar to the soul, i.e. its spiritual content."[16]

Due to its power of animation, the *ethos* of the Greeks, music—and it is this power that gives it the highest title of nobility for the theosophical Ikhwān as for the Sufis—can set souls in flights which are in measured proportion to the receptacle in which they are produced:

> Know, my brethren, that the effects imprinted by the rhythms and melodies of the musician in the souls of listeners are of different types. In the same way, the pleasure which souls draw from these rhythms and melodies and the manner in which they enjoy them are variable and diverse. All that depends on the degree which each soul occupies in the domain of gnosis

213. *Kamāncheh* player; detail from a Persian miniature, Timurid period, 15th century

13. Ibid.

14. Singer/composer, theoretician, and historian as well as jurist (150/767-236/850) who played a considerable role in the transmission of a highly refined Arabo-Persian musical art under the Abbasid Caliphate. His father Ibrāhīm (742-804) was himself a consummate musician. A regular guest of Harūn al-Rashīd, he owned the most richly endowed music school of Baghdad (cf. Farmer, *A History*, 124-126).

15. Cited by G. H. Farmer, *A History*, 156.

16. Cited by G.H. Farmer, *The Religious Music of Islam*, JRAS (1952), 60-65. And also in M.M. Sharif, *A History of Muslim Philosophy*, vol. II, chap. LVII, "Music", 1126.

The following chapter of this last work (LVIII) contains a good summary of musical theories which were expressed at different epochs and in different regions of the Muslim world, such as the influence exercised by Islamic music in other cultural domains.

and on the nature of the good actions which make up the permanent object of his love. Therefore, each soul, while listening to descriptions which correspond to the object of his desires and to melodies which are in accord with the object of his delight, rejoices, is exalted, and delights in the image that music makes of his beloved....[17]

And the Ikhwān conclude their epistle with a justification of the most beautiful and the most perfect music, which is none other than the psalmody of sacred texts:

> Tradition teaches that the sweetest melody which the inhabitants of paradise have at their disposal and the most beautiful song they hear is the discourse of God, great be His praise. It is thus that the word of God Most High states, "The greeting which will welcome them there will be 'salvation'! And the end of their invocation will be: praise to *Allāh*, Lord of the worlds".[18] It is said that Moses—Peace be upon him—upon hearing the words of his Lord was overcome with joy, with happiness, and with rapture to the point of being unable to contain himself. He was overwhelmed by emotion, transported while listening to this serene melody, and from that point on regarded all rhythms, all melodies, and all songs as insignificant.[19]

3—SUFIS AND THE SPIRITUAL CONCERT (*AL-SAMĀ'*)

To listen to music is therefore, in the final analysis, to open oneself to an influence, to a vibration of supra-human origin "made sound" in order to awaken in us the echoes of a primordial state and to arouse in the heart a longing for union with its own Essence. At the beginning of the long chapter of the *Ihyā' 'ulūm al-dīn* ("The Revival of the Sciences of Religion") which he consecrates to the laws governing the spiritual concert (*al-samā'*), song, and ecstasy, Abū Hāmid al-Ghazzālī (1058-1111) writes:

> Hearts and inmost selves are treasuries of secrets and mines of jewels. Infolded in them are their jewels like as fire is infolded in iron and stone, and concealed like as water is concealed under dust and loam. There is no way to the extracting of their hidden things save by the flint and steel of listening to music and singing, and there is no entrance to the heart save by the ante-chamber of the ears. So musical tones, measured and pleasing, bring forth what is in it and make evident its beauties and defects. For when the heart is moved there is made evident that only which it contains like as a vessel drips only what is in it. And listening to music and singing is for the heart a true touchstone and a

214. Mawlawī dervishes

17. *REI* (1966), 192-193.

18. Koran 10: 10-11.

19. *REI* (1966), 192-193.

speaking standard; whenever the soul of the music and singing reaches the heart, then there stirs in the heart that which in it preponderates.[20]

For the person in whom the desire for the good and the beautiful predominates, he who has an ear made for listening to music, it becomes a privileged tool for self-knowledge and interior improvement. Manifesting the latent possibilities of an individual, it permits him to observe, by their movements and their reciprocal interactions, the potentialities of which he was not aware until that moment. A discrimination operates in him, which makes him perceive in his inmost heart, with an acuity in proportion to the quality of the music and to his own receptive capacity, clear and obscure zones of aspirations towards the absolute light, in alternation often with emotional attractions. That this age-old doctrine, already taught by the sages of Antiquity and raised up by generations of Sufis to the rank of a veritable alchemy of the soul, has been transmitted and maintained through to the present time, I hold as proof only a very simple, but significant fact. It is a sentence in Turkish that the father of a contemporary musician who specialized in the songs of Sufi brotherhoods[21] inscribed on the tambourine with which his son accompanied himself. It says: *Aşikin aşkini fasikin fiskini arttirir bir alettir* ("this instrument augments the love of the lover, the hypocrisy of the hypocrite").

The use of the spiritual concert (*al-samāʿ*) as a technique for spiritual realization must necessarily surround itself with conditions and precautions which will guarantee its efficacy and will avoid the strayings and the misguidings of the worldly soul (*nafs*). These conditions are generally the same as those which are demanded of the candidates of the initiatic path (*tarīqah*): moral and spiritual qualifications of the disciple and the acceptance of him by the master (*shaykh*, *pīr*), obedience to the *shaykh*, service to the disciples (*fuqarāʾ*), strict observance of ritual practices particular to the order, as well as those of the *sharīʿah*. More especially, at the time of participation in sessions of spiritual concert (*samāʿ*), dervishes are enjoined to remain as sober as possible and to exteriorize their emotion only when it becomes an ecstatic rapture of an intensity so great that it exceeds all control. Referring to the example of the Prophet Muhammad who, at the time of the first appearances of the archangel of the Revelation, did not succeed in mastering his emotion, Hujwīrī excuses the beginners who, in *samāʿ*, show excitement. He insists that the states provoked by listening be spontaneous:

> You must not exceed the proper bounds until audition manifests its power, and when it has become powerful you must not repel it but must follow it as it requires: if it agitates, you must be agitated, and if it calms, you must be calm…. The auditor must have enough perception to be capable of receiving the Divine

215. The *daira* is used by some brotherhoods to help attain ecstasy, Sanandaj, Iran

216. Member of a brotherhood using the *darabuka* in religious music, Fez, Morocco

20. It is the 8th book of the "quarter" of the *Ihyāʾ* dealing with the "Social Customs" (*ʿādāt*). It has been translated into English by E.B. Macdonald, *JRAS* (1901), 195-252, 705-746 and (1902), 1-28, where the passage cited appears on page 199.

21. This concerns Nezih Uzel, who has given several recitals in Europe and made recordings of Sufi music together with Kudsi Erguner, a player of the *nay*, the reed flute precious to the Mawlawīs.

influence and of doing justice to it. When its might is manifested on his heart he must not endeavor to repel it, and when its force is broken he must not endeavor to attract it.[22]

Abū Hāmid al-Ghazzālī, in the *Ihyā'*, expresses a similar opinion:

> That the participant remain seated, his head lowered as if he were deep in meditation, avoiding clapping his hands, dancing and making any other movement designed to artificially induce ecstasy or to make a display of it.... But when ecstasy takes hold of him and causes him to make movements independent of his will, he is to be excused and must not be blamed.

However, the same master admits that it is certainly not blameworthy to imitate the attitudes and movements of an ecstatic if the intention is not to make a display of a state which one has not attained, but rather to put oneself into a frame of mind receptive to grace.

> ... know that ecstasy is divided into that which itself attacks and that which is forced, and that is called affecting ecstasy. Of this forced affecting of ecstasy there is that which is blameworthy, and it is what aims at hypocrisy and at the manifesting of the Glorious States in spite of being destitute of them. And of it there is that which is praiseworthy, and it leads to the invoking of the Glorious States and the gaining of them for oneself and bringing them to oneself by device. And therefore the Apostle of God commanded him who did not weep at the reading of the Koran that he should force weeping and mourning; for the beginning of these States is sometimes forced while their ends thereafter are true....[23]

217. Player of the double *nay*

22. *Kashf al-mahjūb*, "Chapter on the Rules of Audition", trans. R.A. Nicholson, Gibb Memorial Series (London: Luzac, 1959), 419.

23. *JRAS* (1901), 730-731. The *hadīth* to which Ghazzālī alluded states: "If ye weep not, try to weep", and it is often cited to justify certain Sufi practices, such as the sacred dance (cf. M. Lings, *A Sufi Saint of the Twentieth Century, Shaikh Ahmad Al-'Alawī* [London: Allen & Unwin, 1971], 92-93) (see also note 8 of Part II) .

24. Ahmad Ibn 'Ajībah (1160-1224/1747-1809), his master Muhammad al-Būzīdī (d. 1229/1814) and the latter's master, Mawlāy al-'Arabī al-Darqāwī (d. 1238/1823) belong to the great initiatic line of the Shādhiliyya who, in Morocco, gave rise to numerous ramifications such as the Darqāwī Order founded by the last cited of these three masters.

25. See note 24.

26. See note 24.

Summarizing the teachings of numerous masters of Sufism in his glossary of technical terms, Ibn 'Ajībah[24] describes four successive degrees of approach toward ecstasy. They are:

First, the "seeking out of ecstasy" in which "one affects the appearances of ecstatic emotion and one uses them methodically; thus one employs dance, rhythmic movements, etc. This seeking out is only admissible among the *fuqarā'* who have made vows of total renunciation. For them, there is nothing wrong in simulating ecstasy and in repeating its gestures in order to respond to an inner call.... It is, certainly, the station of the weak but the strong practice it nevertheless, either in order to sustain and encourage the weaker ones, or because they find a sweetness in it.... Myself, when I participated in a session of spiritual concert with our Shaykh al-Būzīdī,[25] I saw him sway from right to left. One of the disciples of Mawlāy al-'Arabī al-Darqāwī[26] told me that his master would not stop dancing until the end of the concert...."

In the second place comes "ecstatic emotion" through which must be heard "that which befalls the heart and takes hold of it unexpectedly, without the man having any part in it. It can be an ardent and anxious desire or a troubling fear...."

Thirdly, "one speaks of 'ecstatic meeting' when the sweetness of the presence is prolonged, accompanied most frequently by intoxication and stupor".

Finally, "if the meeting lasts until the stupor and hindrances dissipate and the faculties of meditation and insight are purified, it becomes ecstasy, the station to which Junayd[27] alluded in this verse: 'My ecstasy is that I disappear from existence, by the grace of what appears to me of the Presence'".[28]

4—THE ELEMENTS OF MUSICAL EXPRESSION

The animating power of music comes, we have seen, from that which it is in essence, a manifestation of the divine Word, a language which reminds man of the state in which, before creation, he was still united with the universal Soul, radiated from the original Light, which reminds him of that instant in pre-eternity when, according to a Koranic saying frequently cited by the Sufis (Koran 7: 172) the Lord having asked souls: "Am I not your Lord?" they answered: "Yea!" It is the memory of this primordial Covenant and the nostalgia for it which music evokes in hearts entrapped in earthly attachments.

There is in music an interpenetration of two aspects inherent in the Supreme Being, *Allāh* (God). One is the aspect of Majesty (*al-Jalāl*) which translates into rhythm, and the other the aspect of Beauty (*al-Jamāl*) which the melody renders. The drum announces the arrival and the presence of the all-powerful King. It is the sign of transcendence, of the discontinuity which separates us, the impoverished, the dependent, from Him, the Highest, subsisting in Himself, while the human voice and the flute sing of the Immanence, the inexhaustible Wealth that no human imagination will ever be able to comprehend but whose every manifestation, mode, or station is capable of becoming a grace and a blessing for the believer.

❧ *Instruments*

Each of the elements of the spiritual concert is invested with a symbolic value and becomes an aid in recollection, in remembrance, in prayer (*dhikr*), for those who are attentive to the language of signs. According to Ahmad Ghazzālī, who taught Sufism approximately a century and a half before Rūmī:

> ... the saints of *Allāh* apply the forms to the realities on account of their abandoning the ranks of the forms and their moving in the ranks of the branches of gnosis. So among them the tambourine is a reference to the cycle of existing things; the skin

218. Members of a Moroccan Sufi brotherhood

219. An Arab with the "monochord", a single-stringed instrument played by the desert people, Yemen

27. The "master of the circle" of the Sufis, who taught and died in Baghdad in 298/911.

28. Cf. J.-L. Michon, *Le Soufi marocain Ahmad Ibn ʿAjība et son Miʿrāj, Glossaire de la mystique musulmane* (Paris: Vrin, 1973), 241-242.

which is fitted on to it is a reference to the Absolute Being; the striking which takes place on the tambourine is a reference to the descent of the divine visitations from the innermost arcana within the Absolute Being to bring forth the things pertaining to the essence from the interior to the exterior.... And the breath of the musician is the form of the rank of the Truth (Exalted and holy is He!), since it is He who sets them in motion, brings them into existence, and enriches them. And the voice of the singer is a reference to the divine life which comes down from the innermost arcana to the levels of the spirits, the hearts, and the consciences. The flute is a reference to the human essence, and the nine holes are a reference to the openings in the outer frame, which are nine, viz. the ears, the nostrils, the eyes, the mouth, and the private parts. And the breath which penetrates the flute is a reference to the light of *Allāh* penetrating the reed of man's essence. And the dancing is a reference to the circling of the spirit round the cycle of existing things in order to receive the effects of the unveilings and revelations; and this is the state of the gnostic. The whirling is a reference to the spirit's standing with *Allāh* in its inner nature and being, the circling of its look and thought, and its penetrating the ranks of existing things; and this is the state of the assured one. And his leaping up is a reference to his being drawn from the human station to the unitive station and to existing things acquiring from him spiritual effects and illuminative helps.[29]

It will have been noted that, in this passage, Ahmad Ghazzālī makes no mention of stringed instruments. That is because he, like his brother, considered them as forbidden "by general consensus" by reason of the frequent use that was made of them in the first centuries of Islam by effeminates for evenings of entertainment hardly compatible with the concerns of men of God. This ostracism, however, was not universal and only reflected the uncertainties which, even in mystical circles, existed in the matter of musical practice. It did not prevent the lute, the *tanbūr* (pandore), the *rabāb* (rebec), and the *qanūn* (zither) from finding their place next to the drums and the reed flute (*nay*) in the oratorios of several Sufi orders such as the Mawlawīs ("whirling dervishes") and the Bektashīs of Turkey, the Chistīs of India and, much later (mid-19th century), the Shādhilīs-Harrāqīs of Morocco who adopted for their sessions of remembrance the instruments of the Andalusian *nawbah*.

In fact these instruments have always been held in the highest esteem by musicologists, who have based scholarly studies concerning the groupings and divisions of notes on them. It must be remembered that al-Fārābī, among others, was himself such a marvelous lutist that he was able, according to his contemporaries, to hold his listeners in rapt attention or to put them to sleep, to make them laugh or cry, and to inspire in them feelings in concordance with his own "moments".

220. Lute (*'ūd*)

221. Dombak goblet drum, Iran

29. *Bawāriq* (cf. note 8 above). Cited by M. Molé, *Les Danses sacrées*, 205-206, and J. Robson, *Tracts*, 98-99.

Such performances are moreover consistent with the theory of the tuning of the lute, formulated by al-Kindī among others, according to which the four strings of the instrument correspond to other micro- and macrocosmic quaternaries such as the "animal tendencies": gentleness, cowardice, intelligence, courage; the "faculties of the soul": memorative, attentive, imaginative, cognitive; the elements: water, earth, air, fire, the seasons, and the signs of the zodiac.[30]

❦ Melodic Modes

The effect that Islamic music, whether vocal or instrumental, has on the soul is directly connected with its modal structure which, technically speaking, is without doubt its fundamental characteristic. In contrast to Western music which has only two modes, the major and the minor, Oriental modes are quite numerous: the contemporary Arab, Turkish, and Persian musicians list them most often as numbering either 32 or 24, twelve of which are very common, whereas during the classical epoch, a hundred were used.[31]

A mode (in Arabic *maqām*[32] in Turkish *makām*, in Persian *dastgāh* or *awaz*) is a type of melody which is expressed by a series of well defined sounds. It is a series corresponding approximately to a Western scale, which does not have to use the same notes for ascending and descending to the octave. Each mode carries a specific name which denotes, for example, its geographic origin such as *hijāz, nahāwand, 'irāqī* or the position of its dominant note on the lute: *dugāh* (2nd position, or A), *sigāh* (3rd position, or B), or suggests the state of the soul or the cosmic phenomenon that the mode is supposed to translate into music: *farahfazā*, "the joyous", *nesīm*, "the breeze", *sabā*, "the morning wind", bringer of longing, *zemzeme*, "the murmur". It is said that the musicians in former times had a precise knowledge of the qualities of the modes and performed them in accordance with this knowledge, exactly as still occurs in Pakistan and northern India where the system of *raga*s obeys rules very similar to those of Persian, Turkish, and Arabic modes. It is thus that they played certain melodies

222. *Above*: The *rabāb* (rebec) is, with the lute ('*ūd*), the principal instrument of Andalusian music

223. *Below left*: On either side: drums used for festive occasions, primarily by women; center: twin drums used in the Andalusian *nawbah* (see p. 112); enamelled pottery from Fez

30. On the subject of these correspondences, which the Arabs systematized starting with Greek sources but which also had roots in the ancient Semites, see H.G. Farmer, *Sa'adyah Gaon on the Influence of Music* (London: A. Probsthain, 1943), 9.

31. On the theory of *maqām* see in particular R. d'Erlanger, *La Musique arabe*, vol. V (Paris: P. Geuthner, 1949); on its current practice in the diverse areas of the Arabo-Muslim world: S. Jargy, *Musique arabe* (Paris: P.U.F., 1971), 49-69.

32. The most anciently used term was *sawt*, literally "the voice", that which clearly marks the principally vocal character of the Arabo-Islamic music during its first period. Later, authors spoke of *tarīqah*, "way", "manner of acting", a term which has also fallen into disuse.

only during certain seasons or at certain hours of the day or on special occasions in conjunction with the places and the ceremonies for which one wished to create a propitious ambience, a spiritual or emotional aura. In the opinion of specialists of Turkish music: "The emancipation of music, its detachment from the complex base of human activities, has certainly taken from *makām* much of its original character, but a portion remains alive, even if it is unconscious. Musicians recognize a *makām* right from the first notes.... Therefore the *makām* always exerts an influence, but only long practice permits one to feel it."[33]

In the mystical perspective, the exploration of a *maqām* by a performer who, on the one hand, humbly adapts himself to the model, to the preexisting pattern which makes up the mode, and on the other hand, improvises a series of melodic passages, of grace notes, and of vocalizations around the essential notes, constitutes a true spiritual discipline. It demands as its basic condition *faqr*, detachment or interior emptiness, and in compensation brings the unveiling of a state or rather a contemplative station, that is to say, in Sufi terminology, a *maqām*, a term which rejoins—and this is not an accident—that of the musicians. Lifted up on the wings of the melody, the musician is able to progress from *maqām* to *maqām*, up to the extreme limits of joy and plenitude, carrying along in his wake those listeners whose hearts are open.

❧ *Rhythm*

The rhythmic structures serve the function of sustaining the melody while providing it with divisions, a temporal framework, and sometimes also a profound and majestic sonorous base. They produce periods of equal duration which, like the meters of prosody, are composed of beats now regular, now uneven, broken and precipitous. The blows themselves are of two kinds, muffled and clear, and their infinitely varied combinations evoke the game of complementary principles such as heat and cold, dry and humid, active and passive, in the sustenance and renewal of cosmic harmony.

The effect of rhythm on the human soul is thus described by a contemporary scholar of the science and sacred art of Islam:

> The rhythm, the meter of the music changes the relation of man with ordinary time which is the most important characteristic of the life of this world. Persian music possesses extremely fast and regular rhythms in which there are no beats or any form of temporal determination. In the first instance man is united with the pulsation of cosmic life, which in the human individual is always present in the form of the beating of the heart. Man's life and the life of the cosmos become one, the microcosm is united to the macrocosm.... In the second case, which transcends all rhythm and temporal distinction, man is suddenly cut off from

224. Drum player from Central Asia

225. Tar player from Central Asia

33. K. and U. Reinhard, *Les traditions musicales—Turquie* (Paris: Buchet-Chastel, 1969), 69-70.

the world of time; he feels himself situated face to face with
eternity and for a moment benefits from the joy of extinction
and permanence.[34]

✒ *The Human Voice*

Among the Arabs as among the ancient Semites, music was an
exclusively vocal art, designated by the word *ghinā'*, "song", which for
a long time served to signify it, before being supplanted by the term
mūsīqā, derived from Greek.[35] In pre-Islamic Arabia, it was in sung
verses that the soothsayers and magicians rendered their oracles and
uttered their incantations. And even if bards and professional singers
played several instruments, these served above all to introduce or to
accompany the sung poems.

The advent of Islam did not change at all the attraction exercised by
vocal music, and song and poetry stayed in honor during the lifetime of
the Prophet as well as after it. It is told, for example, how Muhammad
admitted the presence of singers among his wives or how, while
traveling, he asked some of his companions to sing the *hudā'*, poems
which punctuate the march of the caravans.[36] And when the chronicler
al-Isfahānī reports, in the twenty volumes of his "Book of Songs" (*Kitāb
al-aghānī*) composed in the 3rd/10th century, the acts and gestures of

34. S.H. Nasr, "The Influence of Sufism on Traditional Persian Music", in J. Needleman (ed.), *The Sword of Gnosis* (Baltimore, Maryland: Penguin Books, 1974), 330-343.

35. See *E.I.(2)*, article *MUSIKI*.

36. H.G. Farmer, *A History*, 25.

226. Traditional Berber dancers from the High Atlas, Morocco

the successive generations of musicians up to the Abbassid Caliphate, it is all the cultural life of Arabia and the Near East, before and after Islamization, which he brings to life before our eyes.

For the philosopher and musicologist al-Fārābī, only the human voice is capable of attaining to perfect music, that is, to that which reunites the three virtues of the art of music: the ability to bring pleasure and calm, that of provoking certain emotions and certain sentiments, and that of speaking to the imagination and of inspiring ideas.[37] "Instrumental music sometimes possesses certain of these qualities", concludes al-Fārābī, implying by this that it never possesses them all. He expresses thus a consensus of opinion which has always generally prevailed in the world of Islam, according to which what makes the human voice the most appropriate instrument for the perfect music is above all its aptitude to convey the divine Word. When, in a rare exception, an instrument such as the *nay*, the reed flute of the Mawlawī dervishes, itself also attains by all evidence to the "perfect music", the initiated will explain that this is because it is itself a voice, a breath, that of the human soul which traverses the body, the microcosm purified by love.

227. Turkish miniature depicting Bilāl, the first muezzin, calling the faithful to prayer from the Ka'bah in Mecca

37. R. Erlanger, *La musique arabe*, vol. I (Paris, 1930), 14-16.

5—MUSICAL GENRES

In each of the great ethno-linguistic sectors of the Muslim world—the Arab, the Persian, the Turkish, the Indo-Pakistani (without mentioning here the Malays and Chinese who, because of their distance, have been less permeated by the artistic models of Islam except as it concerns the liturgical arts, the recitation of the Koran, and calligraphy)—the coexistence of three musical genres can be seen:

a) a liturgical, ritual, and devotional music which, in addition to Koranic psalmody whose exceptional importance has already been underlined, includes the call to prayer, the songs dedicated to the praises on the Prophet, and those which, among the Shī'ites, commemorate the martyred Imāms; and finally, the multiple forms of the spiritual concert (*samā'*) with or without dance practiced by mystical circles;

b) a classical music of both an intellectual and sensual nature, the music of the cities, the princely courts, the men of letters and dignitaries, which is especially meant to give birth to diverse nuances of aesthetic emotion but which, given that it rests on the same technical base as the previous one, can show itself capable, if played with the desired intention and in the proper context, of opening the doors of mystical experience to the predisposed listeners;

c) a popular music which, if in general only aims at marking the seasonal rhythms and at celebrating occasions for rejoicing and for mourning, allows itself in many instances to be penetrated by Islam and opens to the common man exceptional possibilities for going beyond his ordinary self.

Since, strictly speaking, only the first of these categories relates directly to the sacred domain, it is this music in particular which will be discussed in the following sections. Among the classical and popular forms of music only those which, adopted by the mystics, found their way into their gatherings, will be examined. By so doing, we will perhaps succeed in evoking the immense richness of the sonorous heritage of Islam and in inspiring the reader to seek out musical experiences which no description is capable of replacing.

↬ *The Call to Prayer* (Adhān)

Instituted by the Prophet Muhammad at the very beginning of the Hegira, the call to prayer (*adhān*) is perhaps, among the exterior signs of Islam, the most powerful symbol of the influence of the realm of the Divine upon the world of man. Chanted five times each day, every day of the year, the call to prayer marks time and fills it. Issued from the tops of minarets towards the four cardinal points, it traverses and fills space, thus affirming the sacred character of these two dimensions in which human existence unfolds. By the proclamation of the formula *Allāhu akbar*, "God is infinitely great", and of the *shahādah*, it places the entire universe under the sign of transcendence. It also likens prayer to "joy", enjoining the faithful to interrupt their ordinary chores or pleasures for a moment of consecration, a veritable preparation and prelude to the beatitude which awaits the believers in the hereafter.

Like psalmody, the call to prayer uses modes of cantillation, that can vary according to the region but in all of which, under a diversity of styles, appears the same homogeneous structure. Those who are charged with giving the call, the muezzins, are chosen not only for their beautiful voices, but also for their human qualities and their piety; sometimes they also perform the functions of the *imām* of a mosque, and most of them participate as singers at religious festivals and spiritual gatherings of the initiated circles.

228. Call to prayer from a mosque in Iran

↬ *Praises upon the Prophet*

The second great source of knowledge after the Koran is the Prophet Muhammad, whose teachings, transmitted in the collections of *Hadīth*, and whose deeds make up the prophetic "custom", the *Sunnah*. If Koranic recitation was able to give birth to different forms of modulated recitation, the person of the Prophet, for its part, has given rise to a great wealth of literary compositions and devotional songs.

The importance of these litanies is linked in Muslim mysticism to the doctrine of the Perfect Man, *al-insān al-kāmil*, for Muhammad, if he is a man, is not a man like others. He is, according to a Sufi saying, "like a diamond among stones". He is also called "the best of created beings" or "the evident prototype", meaning by this that he is the summation of the entire creation, a universal model. To offer prayer upon the Prophet is thus to pray for the salvation of all beings and is also to pray for the rediscovery of one's own primordial nature, to pray for one's own deliverance. Moreover, mystical gatherings almost always begin with praises upon the Prophet. In Syria, in the Qādirī or Shādhilī Orders for example, the gatherings open with a song, performed as a solo, of the *Mawlidiyyah* of Shaykh Barzanjī (d. 1190/1766). The words are notably the following:

> Our Lord Muhammad was always smiling, affable; he never showed the least brutality, the least violence in his words or in his criticisms; he never made a show of his desires and he abstained from judging others and speaking ill of them. When he spoke, his companions kept silent as if a bird had perched on their heads; never did they raise their voices in argument, and when they spoke, it was he who was silent.

229. The whirling dervishes in Konya, Turkey

Another poem also very popular among the Sufis of North Africa and the Middle East is the *Burdah*, the "Cloak", composed in Egypt by Muhammad al-Būsīrī (d. 694/1296), whose title recalls a miraculous healing. Being stricken by paralysis and moribund, in a dream Shaykh Būsīrī saw the Prophet, who enveloped him in his cloak. Upon awakening, he found himself cured and able to move; he carried the poem within him which only needed to be transcribed and which, for seven centuries, has been taken up in chorus by generations of disciples. Rhyming in *mī*, including 162 verses, it lends itself admirably to quick rhythmic variations and, always sung in unison, possesses a great emotional charge.

In Turkey, the meetings of the whirling dervishes, the Mawlawīs, also open with a song in praise of the Prophet, the words of which are due to Jalāl ad-Dīn Rūmī and the music to the composer Itrī (1640-1711 AD), and whose solemnity, reminiscent of Byzantine psalmody, plunges those attending into a state of recollection which prepares them to perform the whirling dance. It says:

> O Beloved of God, incomparable Envoy. . . .
> preferred among all the creatures, light of our eyes. . . .
> Thou knowest the weakness of nations,
> Thou art the guide for the infirm,
> the guardian of the garden of prophecy,
> the springtime of gnosis,
> Thou art the rose garden of religious law and its most beautiful flower.

These examples, which could be multiplied, illustrate the role that Islam, while keeping itself from anything appearing as a divinization of the intermediary, recognized in Muhammad an ever-present spiritual guide, able to help the seeker through his influence and his intercession to approach the Lord of the worlds. A role which, moreover, was not reserved solely for the Prophet but includes, in Sufism, several categories of saints living or dead and in Shīʿite Islam, the Imāms and certain ones among their representatives.

❧ *Devotional Music of Shīʿite Iran*

Among the genres of music which are practiced in contemporary Iran, certain ones show a devotional efficacy and an incontestable mystical resonance.

These are first of all the ceremonial musical styles associated with the great Shīʿite mourning period of *ʿazādārī* which commemorates the Karbalāʾ massacre in which the Imām Husayn and the members of his family were martyred in 680 AD.

These events are recalled in the singing of poems, especially those composed at the beginning of the 17th century by Husayn Wāʿiz Kāshifī in his *Rôzé of the Martyrs* (*rôzé*, from the Arabic *rawdah* meaning "garden"). This collection of poems became so popular that the word *rôzé* serves to designate all the gatherings, whether they are held in a mosque or in a private home, during which the martyrdom of the Imāms is evoked. As for the *rôzé khwāns*, the singers specializing in the recitation of these poems, they are held in high esteem by the population.

The processions of penitents and flagellants which take place between the 1st and the 10th of Muharram, the first month of the Muslim year, are accompanied by songs and exclamations modulated to the rhythm of the march, and are used by the men to punctuate the blows of their fists to their chests and backs.

Finally, theatrical presentations retrace the same tragic events. These sacred dramas are enacted, at least since the 18th century, in the open air in a location which has been specially arranged. This place includes an elevated stage surrounded by an open space for the actors and their mounts. The performance lasts well into the night and includes processions accompanied by songs and the sounds of trumpets, with rhythms maintained by drums and cymbals. The cries of "Husayn, Hassan" return again and again, arousing echoes and tears in the crowd.

Each sequence of the drama is sung in a mode which corresponds to the character of the scene and the person represented.[38] One finds here, therefore, the example of a classical music which was popularized and, in the case of the music of the Āhl-i-Haqq, later became an instructional tool and a source of inspiration for numerous court musicians, particularly in the Qājār period.

Equally specific to Iran is the music of the *zūrkhāneh*, sessions of martial training where the participants wield clubs and heavy chains, spurred on by lyrical songs and powerful rhythms. These take place in a school where corporeal discipline serves the ideal of chivalry such as it

230-231. Musicians from Iran

38. Some examples with musical transcriptions are given by N. Caron, "La musique chiite en Iran", in *Encyclopédie des musiques sacrées*, I (Paris, 1968), 430-440.

was incarnated in the past by Rustam, the hero of the "Book of Kings" (*Shāh-Nāmeh*), and by 'Alī, son-in-law of the Prophet Muhammad and the first of the series of Shī'ite Imāms, whose courage had earned him the surname "the Lion of God".

❧ *The* Qawwālī *of India and Pakistan*

The mystical songs known as *qawwālī* (from the Arabic root *qwl*, "to say") were popularized in India with the Chishtī Order during the 7th-8th/13th-14th centuries. This is attributed sometimes to the patronage of Shaykh Mu'īn al-Dīn Chishtī himself, the founder of the Order (d. 633/1236), sometimes to that of the Sufi poet Amīr Khusraw (d. 726/1325) whose tomb in Delhi adjoins that of Nizām al-Dīn Awliyā' (d. 726/1325), the fourth great master of the Chishtī Order, and it remains to this day one of the preferred meeting places of the *qawwāl*, i.e. the singers of *qawwālī*. In this sanctuary throughout the year one can hear the dervishes singing their religious hymns and poems while accompanying themselves on drums. On holidays real concerts are organized in which eight to ten singers accompanied by various instruments participate, the instruments including the Japanese zither, clarinet, a drum shaped like a cask, the violin, and a small manual harmonium imported from Europe in the last century.

232-233. *Qawwālī* in progress at the shrine of Nizām al-Dīn, New Delhi, India

The lyrics of the songs, sometimes in Urdu and Persian, sometimes in Hindi, are borrowed from the repertoire of the figurative type of Sufi poetry in which evocations of terrestrial beauty such as the garden with its flowers and perfumes, wine, taverns and cupbearers, the face of the beloved and the sighs of the lover, elevate the soul toward contemplation of celestial realities and lead it back to its true existence.

Repetitive formulas drawn from the Koran such as *huwa 'Llāh*, "He is God", often separate the stanzas of the poems and are taken up as a refrain in unison by the audience. Certain poems are, as in the Shādhilī or Mawlawī *samā'*, praises upon the Prophet Muhammad or his Companions and the saints who came after them. Others are connected with the Arabic tradition, and especially the Persian love song (*ghazal*). Here in the ambience of Sufi brotherhoods is a musical art which, while expressing itself at a popular level, is particularly rich through its permeation by the rhythms and melodic modes (*rāga*s) of Hindustani music.

๛ *The Music of the Kurdish "People of the Truth"*

In Iranian Kurdistan (especially the province of Kirmanshah) and in other regions where Kurdish communities are fairly numerous such as Iraq, Turkey, Azerbaijan, and even India, Pakistan, and Afghanistan, there exists a Shī'ite sect of an esoteric nature, the Āhl-i-Haqq or "People of the Truth" for whom music plays an important role during their ritual assemblies. The importance given to listening to music rests in doctrinal and theosophical considerations which are heavily influenced by Ismā'īlism and close to Sufism. They tend to demonstrate that music awakens the aspiration of the believer and links him again to the Beloved, God (*Yār*), with whom an alliance was sealed in preeternity.[39]

Technically speaking, the principal characteristic of this music is the almost exclusive use that it makes of *tanbūr*, a type of long-necked mandolin having two, sometimes three, metallic strings and sixteen frets which when touched with the fingertips give one low sound and one high-pitched sound. The high-pitched sound is used especially for performing solos, the low sound for accompanying song.

Each spiritual guide (*pīr*) should be a musician and, while playing the melodies transmitted by the tradition (certain among them dating, it is said, from the 5th/11th century), he renews the primordial pact in the manner in which the Angel Gabriel, Pīr-Binyānūn, celebrated it originally with the angels and later on the occasion of its earthly appearances.

The assembly includes a series of chanted recitations during which the chanter, accompanying himself on the *tanbūr*, sings religious poems whose refrain is taken up in chorus by those in attendance who, at times, clap their hands to mark the rhythm. They often return to the invocation: "My beginning and my end are *Yār*", in order, they say, "to attract the heart's attention to the divine Principle".

One of the remarkable traits of this music is that it has kept many characteristics of the ancient Iranian tradition, that which the court musicians practiced and which, following several periods of persecution, especially in the late Safavid period, was completely lost. That is why at the present time Iranian musicians and Western musicologists are very interested in the twelve melodic modes as well as in the sacred songs and hymns which continue to resonate throughout the rural sanctuaries of the Āhl-i-Haqq, poems such as this whose first verse invites the faithful to the mystical union:

234. *Tanbūr*

39. The sect has been thoroughly studied by Mohammad Mokri who sets the number of its adherents to be approximately 500,000. See, by this author, *Journal asiatique* (Paris, 1956), 391-422, and (1962), 369-433; *L'Esotérisme kurde* (Paris, 1966); and "La musique sacrée des Kurdes" in *Encyclopédie de musiques sacrées*, I (Paris 1968), 441-453.

The Eternal Hunter, O my soul,
has cast the net of the Pact, O my soul. . . .

❧ *Spiritual Audition of Classical Music*

Throughout the entire Muslim world very close threads have been woven between the mystical path and the principal expressions of classical music, this music having shown itself capable, as the Ikhwān al-Safā' had affirmed, not only of arousing aesthetic emotion but of putting the soul into communication with spiritual realities. The distinction between sacred music, devoted to worship, and profane music was often abolished, and music "for entertainment", with its inseparable constituent of sung poetry, was retained in literary and artistic circles as well as in mystical gatherings. Due to the diverse levels of interpretation to which the majority of Oriental poetic compositions lend themselves, with their metaphorical and allegorical language, numerous Sufi musicians did not hesitate, following the example of the *qawwāl*s of India in the singing of *ghazal*s, to introduce into their concerts "profane" poems charged for them with a supraterrestrial resonance. Inversely, musicians without a particular mystical affiliation appreciated, if not for the profundity of their symbolism, at least for their evocative power and their formal beauty, the works of Sufi poets such as "the Great *Tā'iyyah*" and the *Khamriyyah* ("Praise of Wine") of the Egyptian 'Umar ibn al-Fārid (d. 1234) in Arabic, the pieces from the *dīwān*s of Hāfiz, of Jāmī or of Rūmī in Persian and, in Turkish, those of Yūnus Emre and Ismail Hakki. Thus a breath of spirituality was made to penetrate by means of music as far as the interior of the princely courts and the noble residences of the cities.

The association between Sufi groups and classical musicians was a quasi-permanent characteristic of Muslim society and it continues to the present day. The importance of this can perhaps be illustrated by some examples taken from the great cultural regions of the Islamic world.

❧ *Arabo-Andalusian Music*

In the Arabic speaking world, a constant progression towards "the perfection of musical knowledge", to use the title of a musicological treatise previously cited,[40] was carried on during the initial three or four centuries of Islam. From the mid-2nd/8th century, at the end of the Umayyad Caliphate of Damascus, there existed a formal Arabic music which, being an elaborated version of the popular old recitative, was slowly enriched by Persian and Hellenistic elements borrowed from the new city environments. To ancient poetic meters there came to be added new rhythmic formulas, including the one furnished by the quatrain. The melody had assimilated, in adapting to the Arabic taste, the modal system of the Byzantines and Persians. Finally, to the

235. Two female musicians; detail from a Persian manuscript, 16th century

40. See note 6 above.

236. *Bayād Singing and Playing the 'Ūd before the Lady and her Hand-maidens*, manuscript from Spain or Morocco, 13th century

popular instruments, the reed flute and the single stringed *rabāb*, were added the *'ūd* (lute), the *qanūn* (zither), and the three-stringed violin (*kamāncheh*), as well as several percussion instruments such as the standing drum (*duff*). From that time on, this music had only to reach its full expansion, which came during the long reign of the Abbassids, from 750 to 1258 AD.

Then suddenly came the Mongolian invasion, the destruction of Baghdad, the end of the great epoch of Arabo-Islamic civilization. Some musicians no doubt survived the disaster and continued to transmit their art even in Baghdad and in various Oriental cities. However, it would hardly be possible today to form any kind of precise notion as to what this ancient music was in its plenitude, such as it was analyzed by an Ibn Misjāh, an Ishāq al-Mawsilī, al-Kindī, al-Fārābī and their followers if, several centuries before the Mongol invasion, a branch of this art had not been transplanted from Baghdad to the land of

Andalusia and had not prospered marvelously there before being taken up in North Africa where it has been perpetuated to the present day. The originator of this transplanting was a musician of genius, Ziryāb, who, after having studied with Isḥāq al-Mawsilī[41] in Baghdad, found himself forced to emigrate to Córdoba in order to escape the jealousy of his master. Received with full honors at the court of the Caliph ʿAbd al-Rahmān II in 206/821, Ziryāb there developed an original musical style, although one which was always based on the canons of classical music. Relying on the correspondences established by al-Kindī between the four strings of the lute: 1st (*zīr*, C), 2nd (*mathnā*, G), 3rd (*mathlath*, D), 4th (*bam*, A), the cosmic qualities (cold-humid; hot-dry), the colors (yellow, red, white, black), and the human temperaments (bilious, sanguine, phlegmatic, melancholic), he went very far in the knowledge and utilization of the psycho-physiological effect of musical modes. He added a fifth string to the lute which represented the soul and he elaborated a musical style called the *nawbah*, a style thoroughly imbued with these symbolic perceptions.

A *nawbah*, which could be translated approximately as "suite", contains four (five, in Morocco) melodic and rhythmic movements performed with song and orchestra in an order fixed by Ziryāb and which never varied. There currently exist eleven *nawbah*s, each of which is performed in a particular musical mode such as the major mode (*rasd*) which expresses pride, the mode of lovers (*ushshāq*) which is that of joy and is played in the morning, the *mayā* which evokes the sadness of separation and is played in the evening, or the *ramelmayā*, reserved for the praise upon the Prophet.[42]

Still today, a concert of Andalusian music, whether it be in a light style or a serious style and whether its recitatives are borrowed from classical prosody or popular poetry, or whether, as often happens, it alternates pieces of different styles, it always has a soothing and purifying effect on the souls of the listeners. All vulgarity is excluded and the numerous allusions and conventional but always efficacious images with which it is punctuated—such as the Beloved, the Night (*Laylā*) whose presence is awaited with hope and longing, the garden and its flowers, its fruits and its streams of nectar, the frequently mentioned Friend of God (the Prophet Muhammad) and that of God Himself, named by his "Beautiful Names"—are a constant call to the return toward the source of Beauty which is expressed in the music. And it is why, in Fez for example, since the epoch in which the Merinid sultans patronized the Andalusian musicians, the authorities and the dignitaries of the city have never ceased to encourage the practice of an art felt to be completely compatible with their religious sentiments.

It is also why, despite the rule most usually followed in the cities of the Maghreb, where the performance of instrumental music was excluded from the religious context, some forms of *samāʿ* derived directly from Andalusian music and using its instruments: the lute, the *rabāb*, the tambourine, and the flute, found blessings in the eyes of certain Sufi

237. Folk music performance from Morocco

41. See note 14 above.

42. On the *nawbah* and music of the Maghreb in general, consult J. Rouanet, "La musique arabe" and "La musique maghrébine" in A. Lavignac and L. de la Laurencie, *Encyclopédie de la Musique et dictionnaire du Conservatoire* (Paris: C. Delagrave, 1921-31) and P. García Barriuso, *La musica hispano-musulmana en Marruecos* (Madrid: Instituto de Estudios Africanos, 1950).

238. Dancers and musicians of the Gnawa brotherhood, Tangiers, Morocco

masters. In Tetuan particularly, a city which was a refuge of Andalusian artistic traditions from the time of the final exodus of the Muslims from Spain in the 15th and 17th centuries, an eminently "orthodox" Sufi order can be found, that of the Harrāqiyyah founded around 1845 by Muhammad al-Harrāq, disciple of Mawlāy al-ʿArabī al-Darqāwī, which uses the instruments and the melodies of the *nawbah* to prepare the participants, by having them listen to a series of pieces, for the performance of the sacred dance, which is itself also sustained by a chorus of singers and by beats of the drum.

⌁ *Iranian Music*

Heir to the rich Sassanid tradition, then impregnated by Islamic influences, first Arab and later Turkish and Indian, the music of Iran managed to preserve its personality and its own characteristics throughout the centuries. Its efficacy as a transmuting agent of the soul and the conditions in which it is licit to have recourse therein have perhaps never been explained as explicitly as by the Sufi Rūzbihān Baqlī of Shiraz (d. 606/1209), master of theology, music, and poetry, of whom it could be said he was "one of the *fedeli d'amore* of Islam".[43] All of his written works: treatises, commentaries, and poems, are exhortations

43. H. Corbin, *En Islam iranien*, II, 1972, 9-146; cited by S.H. Nasr, "L'Islam e la Musica secondo Ruzbahan Baqli, santo patrono di Sciraz", in *Sufi, musiche et cerimonie dell'Islam* (Milano: Centro di ricerca per il Teatro, 4, 1981).

to return to the divine Source which calls to man, issuing from Itself, by means of the voice of the Koranic Word and that of spiritual music, the *samāʿ*.

> Sometimes He says, "You are myself", and sometimes He says, "I am you".… Sometimes, He rejects him and sometimes He grants him peace in divine intimacy.… Sometimes He throws him into complete slavery, and sometimes He plunges him into the essence of Lordship. Sometimes He makes him drunken from the Beauty of God, sometimes He belittles him before His Majesty.… All that happens during the *samāʿ* and still much more.[44]

It is the same message that Jalāl al-Dīn Rūmī delivers in his *Mathnawī*:

> The believers say that the effects of Paradise will make every
>   voice beautiful.
> We were all part of Adam and heard those melodies in
>   Paradise.
> Though water and clay have covered us with doubt, we still
>   remember something of those sounds.…
> Sounds and songs strengthen the images within the mind, or
>   rather, turn them into forms.[45]

That the Persians were particularly gifted in composing, performing, and listening to music with a spiritual intention is attested to by numerous historical testimonies. In the contemporary period, despite certain signs of degeneration and ruptures that are probably irreparable, there are musicians to whom it is given to enter into a sublime mystical state and from it to communicate with their listeners. In this state, the artist "plays with an extraordinary facility of performance. His sonority changes. The musical phrase surrenders its secret to him.…"[46] According to another contemporary observer, even if the hardening manifested by the official Shīʿite circles towards the Sufi orders beginning near the end of the Safavid period has more or less discouraged the use of music in mystical gatherings, the content of this music has none the less preserved its spiritual connotations and efficacy: "… there always exists among traditional musicians a certain sense of the sacred". Thus for the master Davāmī, the ninety-year-old depository of a very vast and difficult repertoire, "it is indispensable to have first a knowledge of the hereafter before being able to practice music", this knowledge itself implying a purification of the external senses and the internal faculties which make man to become like a mirror.[47]

Judging by my personal experience, listening to a concert of Iranian classical music demands of the listener the same meditative disposition and leads him along the same paths and towards the same experiences

239. *Kamāncheh*

44. *Risalat al-quds*, Tehran, 1351:54. Cited by J. During, "Revelation and Spiritual Audition in Islam", in *The World of Music—Sacred Music, Journal of the International Institute for Comparative Music Studies and Documentation*, vol. XXIV, no. 3, 1982, 68-84.

45. Cited by W. Chittick in *The Sufi Path of Love: The Spiritual Teachings of Rumi* (Albany, N.Y.: SUNY, 1983), 326.

46. N. Caron and D. Safvate, *Iran—les Traditions musicales* (Paris: Buchet-Chastel, 1966), 232.

47. J. During, "Eléments spirituels dans la musique traditionnelle iranienne contemporaine", *Sophia Perennis*, vol. I, no. 2, Autumn 1975, 129-154.

240. Persian miniature depicting a drinking session in which wine and music lead to ecstatic rapture

as an evening of Andalusian music. Even if the resonances of the voices and instruments are different, those of Iran possessing more mildness and femininity, the melodic and rhythmic structures show so many affinities that one feels oneself transported into the same realm. It is that of the twelve fundamental modes which subdivide into modal figures arranged according to an order established by the greatest masters and in part immutable. It is a world where quality does not consist of innovation and of displays of virtuosity but rather of exposition with fidelity while embellishing with appropriate ornamentation and improvisation the various sequences or figures of the chosen mode. The concert thus takes on the aspect of a gathering of friends where a theme is solemnly introduced and developed, then debated during an exchange of questions and responses, before being meditated upon in a collective spirit in order to finally culminate in the exaltation of a discovery which fills all the listeners with joy.

⤌ *Turkish Music*

The same remarks, or very similar ones, could be applied to the classical music of Turkey, itself not only heir to the Arab, Byzantine, and Persian melodic modes, but also bearer of sounds and rhythms which came from the steppes of Asia and which were for centuries strongly permeated with mystical concerns. In Turkey, in fact, perhaps more than in any other Islamic region, the great religious orders, Mawlawīs, Bektāshīs, Khalwatīs, made much use of music in their ceremonies. The first of these orders particularly, trained a large number of singers and instrumentalists who, while remaining affiliated with the order, became musicians attached to the court of the sultans: such was the dervish Ismail, one of the great masters of classical music, much in favor during the reign of Selim III (1789-1807), and from whom some 150 compositions have been handed down to us.

Performing and listening to a *peşrev* or "prelude", one of the most characteristic forms of Turkish classical music, constitutes an exercise of concentration for the musician, and, for the listener an invitation to contemplative reflection. Composed of four parts, each one followed by a refrain which forms the key for the melodic construction, the *peşrev* is played in one or more modes (*makām*). During its unfoldment, always slow and restrained, accelerating slightly only in the finale, each musician restricts himself to embellishing the fundamental melody at the appropriate places, adding there the conventional grace notes: the *taşil bezek* or "petrified decoration"—a term which also designates the arabesques of architectural decoration—and, at the desired moment, to interrupting the combined movement to perform a solo improvisation. During the sessions of *samā'* of the whirling dervishes, where the *peşrev* has its place, the solo is always given to the player of the *nay*, the reed flute, this voice of the soul in love with the Absolute:

241. A Mawlawī dervish playing the flute

> It is necessary to have heard a *nay* played in a large resonant hall; it is necessary to have seen at the same time the dance of the dervishes, in all its solemnity: to realize the profound inner emotion which is released.[48]

The *nay*, however, is not restricted to the dervishes and whether it accompanies vocal ensembles or is integrated into complete instrumental ensembles including the zither (*qanūn*), the ordinary lute, the *tambūr* (a lute with a very long neck allowing the division of the octave by 24 frets), the violin (*kamāncheh*), of two or three strings and percussive instruments, it punctuates most classical concerts with its nostalgic calls.

48. K. and U. Reinhard, *Les traditions musicales—Turquie*, 105.

❧ *Hindustani Music*

Between Hindus and Muslims in Northern India a remarkable synthesis has taken place in the realm of the art of music, beginning with the growth of Islam on the Indian subcontinent in the 12th and 13th centuries. The first artisans of this meeting were, as we have seen in relation to the singers of *qawwālī*s, the masters and the members of the Chishtī Order who, by the radiance of their faith, brought about conversions to Islam by the score, indeed by the hundreds of thousands. Practicing *samā'* as a method of spiritual realization (Mu'īn al-Dīn Chishtī, founder of the order, considered that "song is the sustenance and the support of the soul"[49]), these Sufis contributed by introducing a number of Islamic elements into Indian classical music, while themselves borrowing extensively from the very rich melodic and rhythmic repertoire of India.

In order for such an interpenetration to be possible, it was necessary that the theoretical and practical foundations of the two musical universes thus brought into contact, the Arabo-Persian and the Indian, be if not identical, at least compatible. To the theory of "influence", *ta'thīr*—that is to say the *ethos* of the ancient Greeks, thereafter Arabized and applied to the Arabo-Persian musical modes—corresponds the theory of Hindu *bhava. Bhava,* the "nature" of the emotion connected to a *rāga* (the musical mode of India), engenders the *rasa,* the flavor or state of the soul particular to this mode. As for the classification of *rāga*s and of their effects and macro- and microcosmic relationships, it surpassed in subtlety even that of the Muslim musicologists. All the conditions were therefore assembled for fruitful reciprocal relations which often had as a theater the princely courts. These courts included that of the Sultan of Delhi, 'Alā' al-Dīn Khiljī, where the Sufi poet, musician, and composer of Turkish origin, Amīr Khusraw inaugurated the style of highly modulated "imaginative" song (*khayāl*) and popularized the Persian love poem (*ghazal*), the court of the great Mughals, especially of the emperor Akbar, where Hindu and Muslim musicians brought to perfection such noble styles as the *dhrupad* which is constructed on rhythmic poems of four verses, the *dhamar,* still more rhythmic, and the *tappā* with its delicate ornamentation.[50]

Even today the performers of Hindustani music are recruited from among Hindu families as well as Muslim families, the latter being able to pride themselves on having contributed to the transmission through generations of musicians of one of the most beautiful musical traditions humanity has ever known. Considering that according to Indian doctrine, "he who is expert in the science of modal intervals and scales and who knows the rhythms, travels easily on the path of Deliverance",[51] and that "at the time of *samā',* the Sufis hear another sound, from God's throne",[52] one cannot doubt that this music was an effective means of reaching inner perfection for the members of the two religious communities. For, as it has been very well expressed,

242. Detail from a Mughal miniature, Lucknow, India, 18th century

49. Cited by J. Sharif, *Islam in India* (London: Curzon Press, 1975), 289.

50. Concerning these different styles, consult A. Daniélou, *Northern Indian Music,* 2 vols. (London and Calcutta: C. Johnson, 1949-1952). The spiritual value of Indian music and the vigor which the music of Mughal India experienced under the influence of Islam have been analyzed in depth in the article by L. Aubert, "Aperçus sur la signification de la musique indienne", *Revue musicale de la Suisse romande,* no. 2, May 1981 (34th year), 50-61.

51. *Yājnavalkya Smriti,* cited by W.N. Perry, *A Treasury of Traditional Wisdom* (London: Allen & Unwin, 1971), 685.

52. Rūmī, *Dīwān* III, 63, trans. W. Chittick, *Sufi Path of Love,* 328.

Music is not only the first art brought by Śiva into the world, the art through which the *asrār-i alast*, or the mystery of the primordial Covenant between man and God in that pre-eternal dawn of the day of cosmic manifestation is revealed; but it is also the key to the understanding of the harmony that pervades the cosmos. It is the handmaid of wisdom itself.[53]

❧ *Popular Music*

In all the regions penetrated by Islam, numerous forms of popular music were allowed to exist or to expand, in addition to the strictly religious music and the great classical currents which we have just outlined. To take an inventory would not be possible in these pages, but we would like nevertheless to cite by means of illustration some cases in which popular music is used for the mystical quest. Sometimes, it is a music with a classical structure which is popularized by adopting the vernacular language and local instruments. Thus the *griha* of the Maghreb, sung in various Arabic dialects: Moroccan, Algerian, or Tunisian, continues the tradition of pre-Islamic ballads based on the airs of *nawbah*s, while the Moroccan, Tunisian, and Libyan *malhūn* is a dialectized Andalusian music, both of them serving to perform innumerable pieces of poetry or rhymed prose composed in dialects of Arabic by Sufi masters.

Throughout the expanse of the *dār al-Islām*, non-Arab ethnic groups integrated Islamic formulas into their repertoires. This is the case of the Atlas Berbers singing the *ahellel*, which is none other than the profession of faith, *lā ilāha illā'Llāh*; or that of the Moorish women of the Western Sahara dancing the *guedra*, the ancient rite of communication with the fecundating forces, while the chorus of men introduces the names of the Prophet and the One God into its rhythmic breathing.

A final example taken from the folklore of Morocco illustrates the very frequent situations in which the music of a village, connected to the cult of a saint, regularly animates religious ceremonies and feasts. The village of Jahjuka, located in the region of Jbala, not far from Ksar el-Kebir, possesses a troupe of clarinetists and drummers whose origin goes back to the time when twelve centuries ago the village was founded by the saint Sidi Ahmad Sharq and his companion, a musician named Muhammad al-'Attār, of Oriental origin. Each Friday, the musicians march through the village to the tomb of the saint, where the faithful come to ask for healing of diseases of the body and soul. The high-pitched sound of the *ghaita*s and the intense rhythm of the drums puts the listener in a state of trance which opens for them the blessed influence (*barakah*) of the saint while facilitating its therapeutic action.[54]

243. Musicians in Tangiers, Morocco

53. S.H. Nasr, "Traditional Art as Fountain of Knowledge and Grace", in *Knowledge and the Sacred*, The Gifford Lectures (Edinburgh: Edinburgh University Press, 1981), 272.

54. To meet the requirements for the production of a documentary film, ethno-musicological research was conducted in the Summer of 1982 in the village of Jahjuka by Philip D. Schuyler, then Assistant Professor of Music, Columbia University, N.Y., who kindly showed me his notes and the synopsis of his film.

EPILOGUE

From each of the areas of classical music as well as popular music flow strong and enduring testimonies showing that these styles of music, like those which serve more explicitly as a vehicle for the words of the Koranic Revelation, the litanies of the pious, or the hymns of the mystics, are an echo of the Beyond, an open path to the liberation of the soul and to its return to the lost homeland, towards the infinite Silence which is the origin of all sounds just as the infinitesimal point is the origin of space and the non-measurable instant is the principle of temporality. Providential instrument of the unification of multiplicity, the traditional music of Islam aids man in realizing by a path of beauty that "in truth we belong to God and in truth to Him we will return" (Koran 2: 156).

244. A woman from Tiznit playing the *rabāb*, Morocco

PART IV

THE WAY OF THE SUFIS

PART IV

THE WAY OF THE SUFIS[1]

1—THE MYSTICAL QUEST IN ISLAM: SCRIPTURAL AND HISTORICAL ROOTS

It has already been shown how Islam has as its first pillar of faith the affirmation of divine Unity and how this is expressed through the profession of faith, the *shahādah*, which makes up the dominant theme of the Koranic revelation. The Koran repeats unceasingly that God is One, without equal, All-Powerful, that He created the world, that He is the Lord of the worlds, the Lord of the Last Judgment, that to Him all things return, that nothing occurs without His will and that everything except Him is doomed to disappear. Between this all-powerful, transcendent, infinite God and the ephemeral, imperfect, and limited creature is there a possible connection? All religions have provided an answer to this fundamental question, and it is an affirmative one, seeing as the word religion itself implies the existence of a bond between the creature and the Creator, religion being that which "binds" man to God. From one religion to another that which varies is not, therefore, the existence of a liaison between Heaven and earth, which is universally recognized, but the modalities through which this bond is realized. This realization can never, obviously, be man's doing. God alone, who created the human being according to certain modalities, with the limitations which make him what he is, can deliver him and efface his individual and separate nature. What man can do, however, is to collaborate with divine action through his intelligence and his will to efface himself, to make room in his heart for the descent of grace, of spiritual intuitions.

In a famous teaching[2] the Prophet Muhammad defined very precisely the type of relationship which is set up between the effort of man and divine action. On that day the Prophet was surrounded by numerous Companions and in this assembly a young man dressed in white appeared whom the Prophet recognized as the archangel Gabriel. This young man posed three consecutive questions to the Prophet corresponding to the various stages of penetrating into the meaning of religion. By the answers he gave to the archangel, the Prophet defined these three stages which are first, *al-islām*, voluntary submission; second, *al-īmān*, faith; and the third stage, *al-ihsān*, perfect virtue, excellence. In defining *islām* the Prophet explained that it consisted of respecting the five pillars which constitute the Muslim religion, that is, witnessing to Divine Unity and the authenticity of Muhammad's mission, prayer, the fast of Ramadan, legal tithing, and pilgrimage. Therefore it is the stage of exterior religion, of submission and obedience, that which asks one to know the prescriptions of the sacred Law and to conform to them. The second stage, that of faith, marks a more advanced step in religious

247. Praying at the Qarawiyyin Mosque, Fez, Morocco

245. *Preceding page*: Page from an illuminated Koran

246. *Opposite*: Frontispiece from a Maghrebi Koran, Spain, 13th century

1. By "Sufi" (adjective and noun) and "Sufism", we mean here that which relates to the interior, mystical, esoteric dimension of Sunni Islam. Although it has certain close relationships with Sufism, Shī'ite mysticism, which includes Ismā'īlī gnosis and Imāmī gnosis is distinguished by specific traits which deserve a special study (cf. S.H. Nasr, *Ideals and Realities of Islam* [London, Allen & Unwin, 1966], chap. VI "Sunnism and Shī'ism", with "Suggestions for further reading").

2. It concerns the *hadīth* called "of Gabriel" or "of 'Umar", in the name of the Companion who reported it. It figures in the collection of Muslim, *Īmān*, I.

experience. It is no longer a question of a simple act of obedience but rather of a grace which enters the heart, which makes one to recognize the foundations of the revealed prescriptions and to adhere inwardly to them with fervor and clarity. As for the third stage, it implies a total commitment of the body, the soul, and the spirit. It entails not only respect for outer prescriptions, not only inner faith but, in addition to these, a total disengagement from worldly concerns at all times and an openness to that which God wills. The man who has come to the stage of *ihsān* is in a way no longer in possession of himself. In fact, according to the words of the Prophet Muhammad to the archangel Gabriel, this stage of perfect virtue consists "of adoring *Allāh* as though thou didst see Him, and if thou dost not see Him He nonetheless seeth thee". The man who is in a state of *ihsān*, the *muhsin*, is truly the *khalīfah*, the vice-regent of God on earth. He recovers "the most beautiful form" in which he was created (Koran 95: 4), because his heart is like a pure, well-polished mirror in which the Divine can be reflected. Leading man back to this station is the goal of Sufi practices.

Another Koranic idea which plays a fundamental role in the mystical quest is that of being completely at God's disposal, the equivalent of the *vacare Deo* of Christian mystics, an idea which is translated by the Arabic word *faqr*, meaning literally "poverty". From *faqr* comes the word *faqīr*, a term which, like its Persian equivalent *darwish*, means "poor" and serves to designate the Muslim mystic. A verse of the Koran (35: 15) says, "O men, you are the poor (*al-fuqarā'*, plural of *faqīr*) before God; He is the Rich!" This saying has an obvious literal meaning, that is, it affirms the infinity of divine plenitude and, in the light of this richness, the state of man's dependence and his utter indigence. But this verse also contains an exhortation and a promise because it is, in fact, in becoming aware of his impoverished condition and in drawing all the conclusions which this implies that man realizes the virtue of humility, that he empties himself of all pretensions including that of existing "at the side" of God or, in the words of the Gospel, that he passes through that narrow gate through which the rich cannot pass and which leads to the Kingdom of God. Such is truly the stripping away to which the mystics, the *fuqarā'*, aspire and it is no different in this regard from that of the Christian Anchorites of the desert or of the *poverello* of Assisi. This same diminutive, moreover, exists in Arabic where the name *al-fuqayr*, "the little poor one", was used for centuries by several Sufis.

According to generally accepted etymology, the word *sūfī* itself is derived from *sūf* meaning white wool, because the clothing made of white wool which was particularly liked by the Prophet Muhammad and by the early disciples wishing to follow his example, very soon became a symbol of ascetic renunciation and orientation towards the contemplative life. A mystic from Baghdad, Sumnūn (d. 303/915), defined the Sufi in these terms: "the Sufi is he who possesses nothing and is possessed by nothing". This definition alludes to two kinds of

248. Sidi Ahmed from Meknes, belonged to the category of "wandering dervishes"; he had friends in many cities and villages of north Morocco

poverty. The first, "to possess nothing", designates material poverty; it is never considered as an absolute condition for coming to God but it is a means, often very useful and even necessary, of achieving inner purification. The second kind of poverty, on the contrary, "to be possessed by nothing", is imperative because it implies the detachment from passions, from desires in which the soul is engrossed and which prevent God from penetrating man's innermost heart.

This observation concerning the woolen clothing worn by the Sufis and from which they take their name provides the opportunity to underline how inherent mysticism is in the Muslim religion and how it has been since the beginnings of Islam. Sufism is not, as some would like to have it believed, something which superimposed itself onto primitive Islam and conferred on it, as a later addition, a dimension which was lacking in the original. In fact, this profound dimension is present in all the pages of the Koran in innumerable verses which teach, for example, that God is near to man, "nearer to him than his jugular vein" (50: 16), that "He is the best and the most beautiful recompense" (73: 20), that He illuminates the hearts of those who invoke Him morning and night with humility, veneration, and love, that He shelters His friends from fear and sadness. In other words God loves to communicate directly through His Word and to provide the means for drawing nearer to Him. And that which He does not state explicitly in the Koran, He makes known through His Messenger whose words and deeds make up the commentary and the illustration of the revealed Message.

By his personality, by his teaching, by the virtues he exemplified, the Prophet Muhammad was the first Sufi, the model which would inspire mystics for all the generations to come. It is from the prophetic tradition, the *Sunnah*, that the Sufis draw much of the directives and counsels which, at all times and in all circumstances, aid the seeker of God in realizing the ideal of *faqr*, spiritual poverty. Even before receiving the Koranic message, Muhammad had made numerous retreats in the mountains around Mecca, especially in the cave on Mount Hira where the Angel of Revelation came to him for the first time, and it is certainly because his soul was already a clear mirror capable of reflecting the truths of Heaven that God chose this man in particular to entrust him with the prophetic mission.

The history of the beginnings of Islam teaches us also that among the first companions of the Prophet were found several individuals of great spiritual scope, in particular Abū Bakr and ʿAlī and the group of ascetics called the "People of the Bench". These people were among the very first emigrants to abandon everything in Mecca in order to follow the Prophet to Medina. They occupied a kind of bench at the entrance to the Mosque of the Prophet in Medina where they spent the greater part of the day and the night, having no other home and preferring to live in this place where they could be near the Prophet and benefit from his teaching as often as possible. To this group in particular belonged the celebrated scholar of Prophetic traditions Abū

249. A member of the Naqshabandiyya Order guards the tomb of Qusam Ibn Abbas, cousin of the Prophet Muhammad, in Shah-i Zindeh, Samarkand, Uzbekistan

Hurayrah, "the father of the little she-cat", whose prodigious memory recorded several thousands of the sayings of the Prophet, and also Bilāl, the black African who, after having been tortured in Mecca for converting to Islam, was saved in the nick of time by Abū Bakr who ransomed him from his tortures. Bilāl was later to become the first muezzin of Islam.

If, over the course of the centuries, Muslim mysticism showed itself capable of integrating the doctrinal perspectives and the elements of spiritual techniques belonging to other cultures, for example, to Neoplatonic Hellenism, to Byzantine Christianity, to the Mazdeism of ancient Iran, indeed to Hinduism and Buddhism, such a capacity for assimilation, far from showing a lack of originality or deficiency, proves rather the vitality of the way of the Sufis and moreover, the universality of the mystical quest, or of that which Frithjof Schuon has so justly named "the transcendent unity of religions".[3]

2—THE WAY TO GOD (*AL-TARĪQA*): CONJUNCTION OF HUMAN EFFORT AND DIVINE EFFUSION

The Muslim mystic, the Sufi, does not passively wait for grace to come to illumine him, even if the coming of this light is always regarded as a spontaneous gift from God. Among the innumerable definitions[4] which have been given to Sufism (*al-tasawwuf*) many put in perspective its operative aspects, the fact that it is a path requiring a strong adhesion of the intelligence and a constant exertion of the will. Thus Maʿruf al-Karkhī (d. 200/813), who was probably the first to define Sufism, said, "Sufism means seizing realities and renouncing that which is between the hands of the created beings".[5] It is an opening, therefore, of the spirit and the heart which leads to gnosis and makes man "one who knows through God" (*ʿārif bi'Llāh*) and is a purification of the soul which renders it free for the manifestation of its Lord by emptying it of futile preoccupation, worldly passions, and selfish desires. Often, the order of the terms is inverted and one speaks of first emptying the human "recipient", the individual "mold" so that the divine Presence, the elixir of Life, the wine of Knowledge can penetrate within.

It is also in this way that the celebrated theosopher Abū Hāmid al-Ghazzālī (d. 505/1111) described the journey of the Sufis, "… they begin by combating their unworthy qualities, cutting their ties to the world, directing all of their thoughts towards God; this is the good method. If someone succeeds at it, divine Mercy is shed on him, the mystery of the divine Kingdom is revealed, and Reality is shown to him. The only effort on the part of the mystic consists in preparing himself by purification and concentration, while maintaining a sincere will, an absorbing desire, and awaiting the hoped-for Mercy on the part of God…. Whoever belongs to God, God belongs to him."[6]

This last formula, in its conciseness, reaffirms the whole doctrine

250. A pilgrim in Morocco

3. F. Schuon, *The Transcendent Unity of Religions*, 2nd edition (New York: Harper & Row, 1975). No student of Sufism can dispense with consulting the other works of the same author, in particular *Understanding Islam* (London: Allen & Unwin, 1976 and Baltimore, Maryland: Penguin Books, 1972), *Sufism: Veil and Quintessence* (Bloomington, Indiana: World Wisdom, 1981, 2006), and *Dimensions of Islam* (London: Allen & Unwin, 1970).

4. If the English orientalist R.A. Nicholson collected 78 of them (in *JRAS* [1906], 303-348), ʿAbd al-Qādir Baghdādī had in the 5th/11th century already collected a thousand according to L. Massignon, *Essai sur les origines du lexique technique de la mystique musulmane* (Paris: Vrin, 1954), 156.

5. Cited by E. Dermenghem, *L'Éloge du Vin (Al-Khamriya), Poème mystique de ʿOmar ibn al-Fārid* (Paris: Vega, 1931), 37.

251. Members of the Harrāqiyya Order, a Moroccan Sufi brotherhood, gathered at Fez on the occasion of the *moussem* (votive festivity) of Moulay Idriss

of *ittihād*, the union between the creature and the Creator which is, for the Sufi, a concrete possibility because he knows that nothing, in reality, is separate from God and exists outside of Him. In addition, it sums up the two complementary and inseparable fundamental aspects of the journey of the mystic: to realize that he belongs to God, that he is completely dependent in relation with Him, the Powerful, subsisting in Himself; and to welcome in his purified substratum the theophanies of the Names and Attributes of the Divinity, the ineffable presence of the Generous, the Dispenser of every grace. The first action includes a voluntary element, the gift of self, the battle of the believer for God's cause "with his riches and his soul", according to an oft-repeated Koranic injunction (4: 95; 9: 20; 41, 81; etc.). As for the second move, that of God giving Himself to man, it can only be the result of a supernatural blessing, a spontaneous unveiling, illuminating the innermost heart with a light which is not of this world and in which man recognizes his true nature.

The desire to achieve the state of ideal poverty and inner detachment, which is the prelude to union with God and its necessary condition, is not for everyone. More often such an aspiration is manifested after years of assiduous practice of religion in its ordinary sense; but it also happens that it occurs as a sudden and irresistible event. That is why, if the religious Law, the *sharī'ah*, is obligatory for all people without exception, or at least for all the members of the Islamic community,

6. *Mizān al-'amal*, cited by A.J. Wensinck, *La Pensée de Ghazzālī* (Paris, 1940), 143-144.

the spiritual Path, the *tarīqah*, does not make the same claim. That is to say it is only for those who are predisposed and called to set out on the great adventure which is the quest for the Divine.

The way which traverses the infinite distance separating man from God is called the *tarīqah*, a term which in fact means two things. On the one hand it means the mystical journey in general, that is to say the sum of the teachings and the practical rules which have been drawn from the Koran, the prophetic *Sunnah* and the experience of spiritual masters. On the other hand, in a more limited sense, the word *tarīqah* (plural *turuq*) signifies a brotherhood or a particular order of Sufis and usually bears a name derived from that of the founder of this order. Such are the brotherhoods known as *tarīqah Qādiriyyah*, founded by Abd al-Qādir al-Jīlānī, *tarīqah Mawlāwiyyah* founded by Mawlānā ("our master") Jalāl al-Dīn Rūmī, or *tarīqah Shādhiliyyah*, founded by Imām Shādhilī. In a certain sense, these *turuq* can be compared to what in Christianity are called the "third orders", those not requiring vows of celibacy or conventional reclusion, but which aim at an ideal which is akin to that of the monastic orders.

⤏ *Initiation*

The Persian Sufi Hujwīrī (5th/11th century) explained that in order to know if one possesses a true mystical predisposition it is necessary that one feels ready to do three things: 1) to serve people, that is, to know how to place oneself at the rank of a servant and to consider each person as a master; 2) to serve God, that is, to cut one's ties with everything which concerns one's present life and even one's future life, because whoever hopes to gain something by serving God is in reality serving his own ego; and 3) to know how to guard his own heart, to maintain it in a state of fervent concentration, in a communion through which the servant proves his desire to devote himself exclusively to the Lord.[7]

When these conditions are realized, the aspirant to the mystical path, can ask to be admitted into a Sufi order by performing an act of obedience to a spiritual master, the *shaykh* (literally "the old one"), *murshid* (guide), or *pīr* (Persian equivalent of *shaykh*). That which the master confers is first of all the initiatic link, the affiliation with the lineage of masters who have succeeded uninterruptedly since the Prophet Muhammad, transmitting both the blessing influence (*barakah*, *sakinah*) necessary for the "greater battle" (*al-jihād al-akbar*) against the inner enemies and the spiritual means appropriate for this battle.

The ritual of affiliation can vary according to initiatic lineage. Most often, it reenacts the handshake given by the Prophet to the Companions when they sealed the covenant of Hudaybiyyah with him under the tree, promising to remain faithful to their commitment to serve God and His Prophet under all circumstances. While renewing this solemn promise the *shaykh*, holding in his hand the hand of the neophyte, recites the tenth verse of the *sūrah* of Victory (48): "Those who swear fealty to thee swear in truth fealty to God; God's hand is over their

252. A dervish from the Mawlawī Order reading Rūmī's *Mathnawī*

7. *Kashf al-Mahjūb*, trans, by R.A. Nicholson, Gibb Memorial Series (London: Luzac, 1911; reprinted 1959).

hands. Then whosoever breaks his oath breaks it but to his own hurt; and whoso fulfills his covenant made with God, God will give him a mighty wage." Frequently at this moment the disciple receives a name which is added to that which he already bears and which becomes the symbol of his second birth into the world of the spirit.

In certain *turuq* the initiatic charge is transmitted by means of a cloak with which the *shaykh* covers the shoulders of the disciple.[8] This cloak might be a patched tunic as among the Darqāwā of Morocco who thus display their disdain of exterior riches. Other ritual objects, such as prayer beads or pages on which litanies particular to the *tarīqah* have been transcribed, are often given to the new *faqīr* at the time of his initiation.

Upon completing the rite of aggregation, which generally takes place during a collective prayer gathering, the *fuqarā'* greet their new fellow disciple one by one and recite in unison the *Fātihah*, the *sūrah* which opens the Koran, so as to commend him for divine solicitude. Sometimes the gathering closes with a communal meal, which seals the entry of the new member into the family in which the *shaykh* is the father and all the *fuqarā'*, brothers, *ikhwān*. It should be noted that since the earliest times women have also followed the path of Sufism and some have even been recognized as spiritual masters.

❧ *The Spiritual Master*

Connection to a master is considered as a condition *sine qua non* for spiritual success. Without a master, without a guide, all illusions, all distractions, are to be feared. This is what is meant by the well-known Sufi adage, "He who does not have a *shaykh* has Satan for his *shaykh*." The true master is, of course, one who has himself already traversed the path, who knows its route, its pitfalls, and its dangers, so that he can guide others. When a disciple has been accepted by a master, he must place himself entirely in his hands and become, according to the saying, "like a corpse in the hands of the body-washer". The goal of this submission is the total effacement of the ego, the psychic death which signals the true birth into the spiritual life.

To illustrate what the relationship between a disciple and his master is, one can refer to the disclosures made by the "very great master" (*al-shaykh al-akbar*) Ibn ʿArabī, who was born in 560/1165 in Murcia and died in Damascus in 638/1240 and who left in his *Risālat al-Quds*, "Epistle on Sanctity"[9] animated descriptions of the spiritual masters whom he had visited in Andalusia, Spain, during the first part of his life. Ibn ʿArabī speaks, for example, of his master Abū Yaʿqūb al-Qūmī and says of him:

> … He was very generous, practicing invocation (*dhikr*) a great deal and secretly distributing alms. He was very gentle with the poor, but he willingly humiliated the rich…. It was rare that one saw him with other than an austere expression; but when he

253. A Sufi master of the 20th century, Shaykh Muhammad al-Hāshimī (see *E.I.[2]*), who emigrated from Algeria in 1910 and lived in Damascus, Syria, until his death in 1961

8. See the article *KHIRKA* in *E.I.(2)* by J.-L. Michon. See also J. Spencer Trimingham, *The Sufi Orders in Islam* (Oxford: Clarendon Press, 1971), 181-193. This work, based on extensive documentation, gives a good survey of the whole of Sufism considered in light of its historical development, its doctrinal variations, its ritual practices, and the organization of the brotherhoods.

9. Translated into Spanish by M. Asín Palacios under the title *Vidas de santones andaluces* (Madrid: Hiperión, 1981) and, in English, by R.J.W. Austin, *Sufis of Andalusia* (London, 1971). The passages reproduced here are cited by T. Burckhardt in *Hermès*, special issue on "Le maitre spirituel" (Paris, 1966-7), (4), 131-132.

254. Shaykh Mulay ʿAlī al-Darqāwī

spotted a poor person, he beamed with joy. I once saw him taking care of a poor person with such tenderness that he had the man seated on his own knee.... Each time I was seated before him or before another spiritual master I trembled like a leaf in the wind, my voice failed, and my limbs stiffened.

Another famous and convincing example of the fruits born by submission to a master is that of Jalāl al-Dīn Rūmī, founder of the Order of whirling dervishes and one of the greatest spiritual masters, as well as poet, the world has ever known. He abandoned his position as professor and the honors he had received in Konya to follow the spiritual teaching of the mysterious Shams al-Dīn Tabrīzī and reached through love of this master and annihilation in him the highest peaks of divine love and contemplative vision.

Seyyed Hossein Nasr has recently defined the function of the spiritual master as follows:

> ... The role of the spiritual master, the *shaykh*, *murshid*, or *pīr*, as he is known in Arabic, Persian and other Muslim languages, is to make this spiritual rebirth and transformation possible. Being himself connected through the chain of initiation (*silsilah*)

to the Prophet and to the function of initiation inherent in the prophetic mission itself, the Sufi master is able to deliver man from the narrow confines of the material world into the illimitable luminous space of the spiritual life....To behold the perfect master is to regain the ecstasy and joy of the spring of life and to be separated from the master is to experience the sorrow of old age.... To become initiated into a Sufi order and to accept the discipleship of a master is to enter into a bond that is permanent, surviving even death.[10]

S. H. Nasr also writes:

… Man may seek the fountain of life by himself. He may seek to discover the principles of spiritual regeneration through his own efforts. But this endeavor is in vain and will never bear fruit unless the master is present together with the discipline which only he can impart. Without the philosopher's stone no alchemical transformation is possible. Only the power of the *shaykh* can deliver man from himself, from his carnal soul, so as to enable him to behold the Universe as it really is and to rejoin the sea of Universal Existence.[11]

Good Company

255. Shaykh Ahmad ibn Mustafa al-'Alawī, founder of the Darqāwiyyah-'Alawiyyah Order, a branch of the Shādhiliyyah Order

That which the disciple finds when he joins a brotherhood is, apart from a master, companions, brothers who, like him, walk on the path of God. The companionship of these brothers gives numerous opportunities for mutual encouragement in the devout life and the practice of the virtues, that is, humility, generosity, and equanimity which lift from the heart the burdens weighing on it and, at the same time, embellish it because they are the reflection of the divine qualities and are, according to the honored saying, "the tongues which glorify the Lord".

In a treatise on Sufism, in which he devotes a chapter to the company of the master, and to fellowship between disciples, Shaykh Shihāb al-Dīn 'Umar al-Suhrawardī (d. Baghdad 632/1234-5), founder of the Suhrawardiyya Order which is widespread in the Orient and reaches as far as India, teaches that the disciple must,

abandon any idea of ownership, live in good understanding with his brothers … love them … show himself to be generous and mindful of the words of the Prophet: "Give to whomever asks, even if he is mounted on a horse", be affable, kind, of an equal temperament…; show a smiling face … don't be secretive and permit no one other than the *shaykh* to elicit confidences; observe the greatest justice towards one's brothers…; maintain a correct balance between excessive austerity and penitence and a too-easy life.[12]

10. *Hermès*, 118.

11. S.H. Nasr, *Sufi Essays* (London: Allen & Unwin, 1972), 57-67.

12. *Kitāb 'Awārif al-ma'ārif* ("The Blessings of Knowledge"), chap. 55. Several editions, including Maktaba 'Alāmiyya (Cairo, 1358/1939). Extracts from it have been translated by E. Blochet in *Études sur l'ésotérisme musulman* (Louvain, 1910) (recently reprinted in "les Introuvables", Paris).

Good company thus becomes the very token of spiritual success. According to Ahmad Ibn 'Ajībah, a master of the Shādhiliyya-Darqāwiyya *tarīqah* (d. 1809 AD), in a letter to a disciple,

> The fruit borne through companionship with men of God is the realization of the station of attainment; and the attainment is that of extinction in the Essence, the station of perfect accomplishment (*ihsān*), the station of contemplative vision wherein the existent is extinguished and only the source of all Existence remains.... If, while living in company with men of God, someone does not succeed in reaching this station, it is because of a deficiency in him: either his aspiration is weak, or his zeal has grown cold, or he has committed an error which causes him to be content with his present state.[13]

And in another letter the same master writes, "It is necessary either that the disciple find the time to get together with his brothers where he is or that he go live near them, or that he visit them frequently in order to know the sweetness of the path and to drink at the springs of realization. Then he will free himself, in God, from all that is not He!"[14]

13. J.-L. Michon, *L'Autobiographie (Fahrasa) du Soufi marocain Ahmad Ibn 'Agība* (1747-1809) (Leyden, 1969; Milano, 1982), 163.

14. Ibid., 160.

256. Members of the Tijaniyya Order at the mausoleum of Sidi Ahmad Tijani, Fez, Morocco

3—THE SPIRITUAL MEETINGS

The advice given to the *faqīr* to make himself free to invoke the name of God communally underlines the importance that Sufism attaches to collective practices. Once initiated, each member can, and even in principle must, attend meetings (*majālis*; sing. *majlis*) of the *tarīqah* which are held regularly at locations and times specified in advance. These are held sometimes on Friday following noon prayers, in the same mosque where the canonical prayer is held, more often in the evening, between the sunset and night prayers, in the oratory—mosque or *zāwiyah*, which serves as the seat of the *tarīqah*, or even in the home of the *shaykh* or of one of the *fuqarā'*.

Although there are considerable differences between brotherhoods in terms of the rules of the meetings, the choice of the texts which are recited and sung, and the techniques of concentration practiced, the same format is found everywhere. It is made up of two parts, the first of which, being introductory, prepares those attending to participate in the incantatory rite that forms the final and essential part of the meeting. The liturgical elements used in the course of the preparatory phase are mainly songs and cadenced recitations performed in an order which forms the "stages" destined to lead the participants from an ordinary state of consciousness to a level of receptivity and fervor favorable to the mystical experience. As for the principal spiritual exercise, that which has the virtue of opening the doors of the "states" and "stations" of the contemplative way for the participants, it can be clothed in different modalities which are distinguished by the respective usage they make of three technical elements: music, corporeal movement, and breathing. Given the important place they occupied, or still do occupy, in the spiritual life of the Muslim community, two major types of incantory rites will be discussed here. They are, first, the most widespread among the *turuq* such as the Qādiriyyah and Shādhiliyyah, based on the rhythmic repetition of the divine Name *Allāh*, and the second which is the "spiritual concert" (*samā'*), the most justly celebrated example of this being found in the Mawlāwiyyah (Mevlevīs in Turkey) or "whirling dervishes", characterized by the use of music and the technique of a turning dance.

Before beginning a description of the various components of the mystical gathering, it is, however, necessary to pause for a moment upon the thread which connects them and which forms the woof of the gathering as it weaves together all the instants of the life of each true *faqīr*. This guiding thread is the remembrance, the invocation of God.

257. *Dhikr* session in Baghdad, Iraq

15. The immense body of literature treating the *dhikr* cannot be summarized here. One could consult the article *DHIKR* of *E.I.(2)* (L. Gardet) and, especially, the few pages which T. Burckhardt consecrates to this topic in his illuminating *Introduction to Sufi Doctrine* (Bloomington, IN: World Wisdom, 2008), 89 ff. See also M. Lings, *What is Sufism?* (London: Allen & Unwin, 1975), chap. 7, "The Method" and W. Stoddart, *Sufism: The Mystical Doctrines and Methods of Islam* (Wellingborough: Thorsons, 1976), 64-70.

✺ *Invocation* (al-Dhikr)[15]

Wa ladhikru 'Llāhi akbar, "the *dhikr*"—remembrance, recollection, mindfulness, naming, or invocation—"of *Allāh* is greater" or "the greatest thing". With these words the Koran (29: 45) states the primacy of

258. The ninety-nine Names of *Allāh*

259. *Hadīth*: "There is a way of polishing everything and removing rust and that which polishes the heart is the invocation of God"; calligraphy by Muhammad Zachariah

16. Especially by Abū Hāmid al-Ghazzālī who made of this one of the major themes of "The Revival of the Sciences of Religion" (*Ihyā' 'ulūm al-dīn* [Cairo, 1352 H.], III). Likewise, in the contemporary period, the Algerian Sufi Ahmad al-'Alawī (d. 1934) explained all the religious prescriptions of Islam in terms of their value for *dhikr*. On this subject see *Al-minah al-quddūsiyya fī sharh al-Murshid al-mu'in bi tarīq al-sūfiya*, (Tunis, 1324 H.), extracts of which have been translated by M. Lings in *A Sufi Saint of the Twentieth Century*, chaps. X and XI.

the *dhikr* (invocatory prayer) both in terms of relative value in relation with other ritual prescriptions such as the canonical prayer mentioned in the preceding verse, and in terms of absolute value, the invocation being affirmed as the path of salvation *par excellence*. To perform *dhikr*, to invoke, is to "pray unceasingly," saying a Divine Name or sacred formula repeatedly. Doctrinally speaking, the *dhikr* is the becoming aware by the creature of the connection which unites him for all eternity to the Creator. Seen in this way, the invocation constitutes the very essence of religion, as much in its exoteric dimension (where man remembers God as his Master and transcendent and omnipotent Judge) as in the esoteric order (where the divine Presence reveals itself within the human being). From an operative and theurgical point of view, each of the means that the Revelation has placed at the disposal of believers in order to help them to attain this awareness is *dhikr*. There are, on the one hand, ritual practices which are obligatory for all of the faithful, those which are connected to the five pillars of Islam and whose powers of recollection have often been commented upon by the mystics.[16] Next come the supererogatory deeds that the most devout Muslims, Sufis or non-Sufis, are able to carry out *ad libitum* to get nearer to their Lord, such as the reading of the Koran, preferably during the night, the voluntary fasting and almsgiving, and the numerous prayers and rogations recommended by the *Sunnah*. There are, finally, in the Sufi cadre, spiritual exercises based on the repetition and contemplative penetration of certain Koranic formulas, especially those which contain the Names of the Divinity.

Numerous verses of the sacred Book recommend multiple performances of invocatory prayer (*dhikr*), invoking God morning and night, in fear and humility, until the soul is appeased. The following are some of these injunctions:

"Call upon God, or call upon the Merciful; whichsoever you call upon, to Him belong the Names Most Beautiful" (17: 110).

"Remember Me, and I will remember you", or "Mention me, and I will mention you" (2: 152).

"O believers, remember God oft, and give Him glory at the dawn and in the evening. It is He who blesses you, and His angels, to bring you from the shadows into the light. . . ." (33: 41-43).

"… in temples God has allowed to be raised up, and His Name to be commemorated therein; therein glorifying Him, in the mornings and the evenings, are men whom neither commerce nor trafficking diverts from the remembrance of God and to perform the prayer, and to pay the alms…" (24: 36-37).

"God guides to Him … those who believe and whose hearts are at rest in God's remembrance because surely, in God's remembrance are hearts at rest" (13: 27-28).

Some sayings of the Prophet as recorded by his disciples have the same import:

"Men never assemble to invoke *Allāh* without being surrounded by angels and covered by divine Blessings, without peace (*sakīnah*) descending on them and *Allāh* remembering them."

"There is a way of polishing everything and removing rust and that which polishes the heart is the invocation of God."

"'Shall I tell you the best of your deeds? The purest toward your King, that which most elevates you in degree, whose accomplishment is more beneficial than the act of giving (by way of alms) gold and silver or of meeting your enemy and striking him down or being struck?' The Companions said, 'Tell us.' The Prophet answered, 'It is the invocation of God the Most High'" (al-Tirmidhī, as told by Abū'l-Dardā').

Among the numerous formulas employed in invocation, certain ones have always found favor among the Sufis. Thus "the most beautiful Names" mentioned in the Koran, from which a list of 99, corresponding to the number of beads on the rosary, are recited individually or collectively, each Name being followed by the formula *jalā jalāluhu*, "that His Majesty shine forth", meaning that each of the divine Qualities is a ray of that infinite Glory which is in itself an unattainable Mystery.

The majority of the divine Names taken individually can also be made the object of a *dhikr*, just as several Names possessing special affinities in common can be associated in the formulas of invocation. Some of these groupings are *yā Hayy, yā Qayyūm!* (O, Living, O Immutable!), *yā Rahmān, yā Rahīm!* (O Merciful, O Forgiving), and similarly the *basmalah*, the formula for consecration "in the Name of God", which contains the latter two Names.

The repetition of the first part of the profession of faith, *lā ilāha illā 'Llah*, is universally practiced in mystical circles, in conformity with the teaching of the Prophet, "the best invocation is 'There is no god but God'" (al-Tirmidhī, as told by Jābir). Its particular effectiveness comes from evoking the two phases of spiritual realization, negation of all "divinity", that is, of any secondary reality not having its own sufficient reason, and affirmation of the sole Reality of the Absolute Being; effacement of the creature and return to the Creator; annihilation of the separate self and reunification with God.

However, the invocation *par excellence* is that of the Name *Allāh*, the non-qualified name of the Divinity, also called the Supreme Name, the Unique Name, and the Name of Majesty. With its symbolic two syllables and four letters,[17] this Name concentrates all the redemptive efficacy of the divine Word. "God is present in His Name", say the Sufis. To the degree that, through the conjunction of this Presence and a serious concentration on the part of the invoker, he finds himself effaced, absorbed in the One Invoked, the *dhikr* becomes God's *dhikr* alone, in which the invocation, the invoked, and the invoker are one with the One without second.[18]

Given its incomparable grandeur, the invocation of the Supreme Name can only be practiced under certain conditions, with the authorization of the *murshid* and under his control. Thus, the authorization to practice invocation outside of collective gatherings is not generally granted to the disciple at the time of his entry into

260. The Divine Name, *Allāh*

261. "There is no god but God" (*Lā ilāha illā 'Llah*); calligraphy by Khurshid Alam

17. See especially F. Schuon, *Understanding Islam* (Baltimore, Maryland: Penguin Books, 1972), 122-128.

18. Doctrine developed with great clarity by Ibn 'Atā' Allāh of Alexandria, the third great master of the Shādhilī Order (d. 709/1309) in his treatise entitled *Kitāb miftāh al-falāh wa misbāh al-arwāh* ("The Key of Felicity and the Lamp of Souls") (Cairo: Mustafa al-Bābī al-Halabī, 1381/1961), 143. The introduction to this treatise has been translated into French by M. Gloton, *Traité sur le Nom Allāh* (Paris: Les deux Oceans, 1981), 209-220.

the *tarīqah* but at a later stage, when the *shaykh* has sufficiently tested the disciple's qualifications and has recognized in him the quality of "traveler" on the mystical path and not only that of being "affiliated with the blessings" which surround the *tarīqah*.

The right to invocation thus constitutes for the *faqīr*, according to the saying of Abu Alī al-Daqqāq, master and father-in-law of Qushayrī (d. 465/1072), the "symbol of initiation", so that "he who receives the *dhikr* is enthroned, while he who loses it is dismissed".[19]

If such precautions are necessary to avoid the dangers to which novices could expose themselves by wrongly performing *dhikr*, they are not needed at collective sessions where the presence of the *shaykh* and of older and experienced *fuqarā'* provides a guarantee and a security against excesses and other undesirable psychic manifestations to which the beginners on the Sufi path could be subjected.[20]

❧ *The* Wird

The spiritual meeting opens with a collective recitation, in a loud and rhythmic voice, of the *wird* (the Muslim "rosary"), sometimes called *hizb* or *wazīfa*, which is the litany proper to the brotherhood. Made up essentially of a series of formulas taken from the Koran which, individually, are repeated a certain number of times 3, 7, 10, 29, 33, 100, or 1000 times, the *wird* represents a symbol for the *fuqarā'* of their connection with the initiatic chain (*silsilah*) going back to the Prophet, with the master who brought them into the *tarīqah* being the most recent link. To recite the *wird* is, in a sense, to renew the pact made with the *shaykh*, with the Prophet, and with God Himself. And it is also, symbolically at least, to traverse the entire distance of the spiritual path, the order in which the formulas are arranged having been conceived to retrace the principal steps to the approach towards God.

Thus, the *wird* of the Qādiriyyah, the first to be recorded from the great Sufi Orders, founded in the 6th/12th century by 'Abd al-Qādir al-Jīlānī, like that of the Shādhiliyyah (7th/13th century) always include at least one hundred repetitions of the following formulas: a) the plea for forgiveness (*istighfār*), b) the prayer upon the Prophet (*salāt 'alā' n-nabī*), c) the testimony of faith (*shahādah*).[21] These formulas correspond to fundamental spiritual attitudes which each aspirant to the mystical life must assimilate. They are:

1. the station of fear of God (*makhāfah*) which implies repentance (*tawbah*) and renunciation of worldly pleasures;

2. the station of love (*mahabbah*) which implies patience and generosity, qualities which were united in an exemplary fashion in the person of Muhammad; and

3. the station of gnosis (*ma'rifah*), that is, of discernment and of concentration on the divine Presence.

The Sufis also establish a concordance among these three formulas and the three stages of religion mentioned in the *hadīth* called "from Gabriel": the stage of *islām* which engages the external faculties and

19. Cited by Ibn 'Ajībah in *Mi'rāj al-tashawwuf ilā haqā'iq al-tasawwuf*, French translation in J.-L. Michon, *Le Soufi marocain Ahmad Ibn 'Ajība (1746-1908) et son Mi'rāj, Glossaire de la mystique musulmane* (Paris: Vrin, 1973), 215.

20. For a description of the modalities and techniques applied in the two "traditions" of the solitary *dhikr* and the collective *dhikr* see L. Gardet, "La mention du Nom divin en mystique musulmane", in *Revue Thomiste* (1952), III, 648-662.

21. The repetition of these formulas has its foundations in the prophetic tradition. Thus, the Prophet said, "There is not a servant male or female who has said seventy times each day, 'I ask forgiveness from God' without God having pardoned him or her of seven hundred sins; the loser is the servant who would commit in one day and one night more than seven hundred sins" (al-Bayhaqī in *Shu'ab al-imān*, according to Anas).

Anas heard the Prophet say, "… whoever prays to me one hundred prayers, God inscribes between his two eyes innocence from hypocrisy and safeguard from hell; on the Day of Judgment, He places him with the martyrs" (Tabarānī).

"Never has a servant said, 'There is no god but God, Unique, without equal, to Him the Kingdom, to Him the praise, and He is All-Powerful above every thing', with pure adherence of spirit, sincerity of heart, and pronunciation of the tongue, without God opening wide the heavens to look down upon the one who speaks thus from the earth; and the one whom God looks down upon will see seeing his prayers granted" (Nasal); according to *Majmū al-awrād*, compiled by 'Uddah ibn Tūnis, 2nd ed. (Damascus: Matba'a At-tawfīq, 1350/1932).

consists in carrying out the prescriptions of the religious Law (*sharī'ah*) and in abstaining from that which it forbids; the stage of *īmān*, which is accessible through the internal faculties, and which demands steady progressing along the mystical path (*tarīqah*) and the total surrendering of oneself; and finally the stage of *ihsān*, wherein the divine Light penetrates and illuminates the innermost core of beings, becoming the place where total Reality (*haqīqah*) is unveiled. The first stage is that of the common people, the second that of the elite, the third that of the elect among the elite, the gnostics who have "attained" God.

✧ The Hymns

The recitation of the *wird*, which lasts about a half-hour, is sometimes followed by a brief period of spiritual exhortation during which the *shaykh* reads and comments upon some passage of a treatise on Sufism or exposes an aspect of the mystical path and then answers disciples' questions concerning the subject discussed.

262. *Dhikr* session in Aleppo, Syria

After this comes the part called the spiritual "audition", (*al-samā'*) which includes first the performance of several sacred songs taken from the vast repertoire of Sufi poetry: odes and quatrains from Arab, Persian, or Turkish poets, or poems in the local dialect often composed by anonymous bards. One very popular category of hymns is made up of praises which traditionally celebrate the anniversary of the birth of the Prophet the 12th of Rabi' al-Awwal of each lunar year but which, for the past century, have gradually been introduced into the ordinary meetings of the *turuq*.

At their gatherings, the Shādhilī dervishes of Syria, whose order is representative of a large number of initiatic circles, sing, among others, hymns drawn from the collection of poems (*Diwān*) of the Sufi 'Abd al-Ghanī al-Nābulusī (from Nablus, in Palestine) who lived from 1641 to 1731. Here are some of the verses that a young *munshid* with a beautiful voice sang not long ago (1964) in a *zāwiyah* in Hama; unfortunately, only the meaning of the words can be given, translation being unable to convey the harmony and the rhythm of this canticle:

O thou who appearest at the rising of the spheres of the
    Invisible,
O thou who stoppest in the tent of the men of the heart.
Do not blame me, o censor, for loving the beautiful ones with
    supple bodies,
Since I have no other attachment but towards the One who is
    present behind the veils.
The perfume of secrets is exhaled from the garden of the meeting,
    And its emanations have made us drunk.

This piece is typical of the symbolic images used by the Sufi poets, be they Arab or Persian. Thus, "he who stops in the tent of the men of the heart" is the intellect, the first Intellect which the Sufis consider to be the first created thing and therefore, like the ray of light which unites all the worlds. "The beautiful ones with supple bodies" are the incorruptible beauties of the subtle world, the houris, who are for the mystic irradiations from the Absolute Essence. "The perfume of secrets" are the tangible manifestations of the divine Presence, each of which intoxicates because it brings to the heart the light and warmth of this Presence, itself often associated with wine[22] or with Layla, the Beloved.

As for the evocation of the Prophet which is also made in the form of sung poems, it possesses the same virtue as the *salāt* (prayer) contained in the second formula of the *wird*: Muhammad, "the best of created beings", "the evident prototype" is the channel through which divine benediction descends on earth and spreads among men; he is the intermediary for anyone wishing to return to the very source of benedictions, the prayer to him leading to the Lord by a path of love and beauty.

Thus in their weekly gatherings of recollection the *fuqarā'* of the Shādhilī Order from Morocco to Iraq sing in unison verses from the *Burdah* ("the Coat"), of the Egyptian Shaykh al-Būsīrī such as this one: "When you see him, to him alone is demanded respect equal to that for an escort, or for any army"; or again, some extracts from the *Hamziyyah* (a poem rhyming with *hamzah*) in which the same author, after having described the virtues of the Prophet, concludes: "The image that men can give of these qualities is none other than that of the stars reflected in water."

It is a fact that the hymns dedicated to the Prophet never fail to create a climate of intense fervor in which the listeners commune with the beloved and, through contact with him, are stripped of their egotistical pretensions and prepared to enter into the rite which is the heart of many a Sufi meeting: the ecstatic dance.[23]

263. *Dervishes Dancing*, miniature from the *Khamsah* of Amir Khusrau, 1485

✦ *The Sacred Dance*

The majority of the *turuq* possess a mode of collective invocation which lends itself to corporeal movement. The Mawlawīs, the whirling dervishes, call it *samā'*, spiritual audition, because it pertains to a rite in which dance is sustained by a complete musical ensemble—vocal, instrumental, and rhythmic—the music itself being considered as a form of invocation. Other *turuq* such as the Qādiriyyah and the Shādhiliyyah speak rather of *hadrat al-dhikr*, meaning literally "presence of invocation", because the Name which is pronounced in the meetings is the Name of God Himself, *Allāh*, the Name in which God is present and through which He makes Himself present. Pronouncing the Divine Name, on which the rhythm of the *hadrah* (sacred dance) is based, is thus a sacrament in the strictest sense of the term, that is, a supernatural act which allows man to leave his nature and to be transformed, absorbed in a dimension which surpasses him. In the Maghreb

22. As in the famous *Khamriyyah* of the Egyptian Sufi 'Umar Ibn al-Fārid (d. 632/1235), a poem for which 'Abd al-Ghanī Nābulusī wrote a commentary. See E. Dermenghem, *L'Éloge du Vin* (*Al-Khamriya*), trans. with the commentary of Nābulusī (Paris: Vega, 1931).

23. Cf. the examples of "Praises on the Prophet" (*amdāh nabawiya*) already quoted above (pp. 105-107) in connection with ritual music.

where there are numerous branches of the Shādhilī Order such as the 'Isāwiyyah, the Zarrūqiyyah, the Nāsiriyyah, the Darqāwiyyah, etc., this form of sacred dance is also called *'imārah* or "plenitude" because the name of the Divine Essence, *Allāh*, or simply *Huwa*, He, in penetrating the human receptacle, fills it beyond measure.

In fact, the dance of the Sufis has nothing in common with either that which the word "dance" signifies in the West, or even with the traditional forms of Oriental and Far Eastern sacred dance, such as that of the Brahmanic temples or the Shinto sanctuaries, for example, where the protagonists mime and play the parts of supernatural powers. Nor is it a representation since in principle only the actors take part in it, spectators not being admitted to gatherings except in exceptional cases, such as that of relatives or sympathizers wishing to benefit from the blessed ambience which issues from the gathering.

The movements which make up a *hadrah*, different according to the brotherhood, are reduced to a few fairly simple motions. According to the explanations given by the Sufis, in the beginning of the dance there is usually a spontaneous movement, of the same nature as that elicited by the arrival of good news. It is thus that the words of the Prophet addressed to certain of his Companions would have caused physical expressions of overflowing joy which, imitated by other Companions and repeated from generation to generation, would be at the base of the *hadrah*. An ecstasy of Abū Bakr was to give birth to the whirling dance practiced by the first groups of Sufis before becoming the preferred rite of the Mawlawīs. Another of Ja'far ibn Abī Tālib was to be carried on in the leaps into the air to which numerous brotherhoods of *fuqarā'* give themselves over, particularly the Qādirī or Shādhilī Orders.[24] Other movements such as the rapid lowering of the upper part of the body passing from a vertical position to a horizontal one and then returning quickly to the vertical in an increasingly rapid rhythm, or the rotation of the head alternatively to the right and to the left, derive without doubt from the motions of the canonical prayer while at the same time appear linked to the punctuation of the Semitic speech, which provoke a spontaneous rocking of the body during Koranic psalmody or Judaic prayer.

In the case of sacred dance, as in that of music itself, it proceeded to graft onto the ancient Arabo-Semitic base, already enriched by the coming of Islam, some ethnic elements that the Sufis adopted because these elements responded to their own concerns: rhythms of African singers entered into the Moroccan brotherhoods, the 'Isāwiyyah for example, by way of converted black slaves,[25] fragments of shamanistic ritual were integrated, it is said, into the *samā'* of the whirling dervishes,[26] breathing techniques were taken from Christian monks or Hindu yogis etc. The mystic path, by the same definition, has no borders and the identical end sought by the seekers of God justifies the sharing of their means.

Whatever their methods, the dances of the dervishes all concur on

264. Detail from an illustration to Rūmī's *Mathnawī*, Herat, Afghanistan, 1458-1459

24. We have already seen the explanation of the symbolism of these gestures given by Ahmad Ghazzālī in his *Bawāriq* (above pp. 99-100 and note 29 of Part III).

25. See the article *'ISAWIYYA* in *E.I.(2)* (J.-L. Michon).

26. According to M. Köprülüzade, "Influ-ence du chamanisme turco-mongol sur les orders mystiques musulmans", *Mém. Institut de Turcologie Univ. Stamboul, N.S.I.* (1929).

the same goal, which identifies itself with other Sufi practices and is summed up in the single word *dhikr*, recollection, remembrance of the Divine, ending in the effacement of the creature and in his being taken over by the Being who knows no limits. Sometimes this "state of being" or "ecstasy" already exists at the beginning of the dance and this dance then is only the incoercible, spontaneous, and exterior manifestation of an interior state. Sometimes the dance appears like an "effort of seeking" which, according to the predisposition of the dancer, may or may not lead to a veritable ecstatic experience.[27] In all the cases, the ideas of spontaneity, simplicity, and absence of affectation reappear constantly in the teaching of the masters, who stress their importance in the validity of the *samā'* and its efficacy. Wishing to exculpate themselves and their disciples from the accusation of hypocrisy hurled by the exoteric scholars, who accuse them of feigning ecstasy, certain masters went so far as to say that the dance should only begin when one or more dervishes had already entered into a state of rapture and become incapable of controlling themselves. At this moment their "brothers" had the duty of rising and joining them in the ecstatic dance. Most often, however, it is the enthusiasm of the dervish himself, his desire to give himself to God, which is taken as the criterion of sincerity and which, for the dervish, constitutes the authorization to throw body and soul into the *samā'* and, with the help of Grace, to reach the desired goal, the extinction of self, the inner illumination.

Due to its collective character, which may be noisy as in the case of the "howling dervishes", and, especially in the case of the Mawlawīs, quite spectacular, the ecstatic dance has been not only criticized but, in numerous instances, forbidden by religious or secular authorities. It continues however in numerous Sufi Orders such as the Rifā'iyyah and Sa'diyyah in Syria and Egypt and the Qādiriyyah and Shādhiliyyah which span all of the Muslim world, often clothing itself in more discrete forms or dissimulating itself with more or less success under the aspect of cultural or folkloric manifestations, as in the case of the Mawlawīs in modern, secular Turkey or the 'Isāwiyyah of the Maghreb.[28]

There are numerous ways of invoking the name *Allāh*. The invocation can be silent, scarcely audible, or it can be uttered aloud. The Name can be pronounced slowly or quickly and rhythmically. The most widely used method of invocation, that of the Shādhilī or Qādirī *hadrah*, is rhythmic, called "the invocation from the chest" (*dhikr al-sadr*) because after having begun by pronouncing the name *Allāh* in its entirety with all its letters, the participants finish by pronouncing only the final *hā*, in a breath which no longer uses the vibration of the vocal chords but only alternating contraction and expansion of the chest.

At the start of this rhythmic invocation, all the participants stand side by side and join hands, forming one or more either concentric circles or rows facing one another. In the center stands the *shaykh* or one of his assistants. This arrangement, which is also found among the whirling dervishes, evokes the symbolism of the circle of angels,

265. Bandir player, participating in a *dhikr* session of a Sufi brotherhood in Meknes, Morocco

27. The question of the relationships between *dhikr* and *samā'* and the primacy which, depending on the period and the school, was given to one or the other of these two is examined by F. Meier, "Der Derwischtanz" in *Études Asiatiques*, 22 (1954), fasc. 1-4, 107-136.

28. For a more detailed inventory of these brotherhoods, consult L. Massignon and V. Monteil, *Annuaire du Monde musulman* (Paris, 1954) and J. Spencer Trimingham, *The Sufi Orders of Islam* (London: Oxford University Press, 1971).

or the rows of angels which surround the divine Throne. The session begins with a slow rhythm. The dancers pronounce the divine Name in unison, bowing the trunk of the body rapidly and fully at the moment of exhaling the second syllable, *lāh*. When they inhale, they stand erect again. The rhythm increases in tempo little by little, and the movements of the body always accompany the two phases of the breath. The name *Allāh* is soon no longer clear and only the last letter *hā* remains, which all the chests exhale in an immense burst of air. Each of these exhalations symbolizes the last breath of man, the moment when the individual soul is reintegrated into the cosmic breath, that is to say, into the divine Spirit which was blown into man at the time of creation and through which man always remains in communication with the Absolute. Keeping with the movements of the chest, the body is alternately lowered and raised as if at each instant it were being pulled toward the sky and then sent back toward the earth. All the eyes are closed; the faces express a kind of painful rapture. One need not fear pointing out that if the breathing of this *dhikr* evokes a rapture of a more sensual order, it is not an accident. There are precise correspondences between the higher order and that here below and that is why for example, earthly love is able to serve as the point of departure for the realization of divine love, and it is also why the houris of paradise symbolize the delights of heaven.

The Mawlawī session, the *samā'*, is also entirely woven from symbolic elements which all concur on the same goal, the *dhikr*, the call to the Divine. The very costume of the dancers is charged with significance. Their headgear, a large tarboosh of brown felt, represents the vertical dimension, the axis which escapes the tribulations of desire and passion; it also represents the tombstone and reminds the wearer of the unavoidable door of death, the ephemeral nature of this lower world, and of the necessity for seeking in this life the Truth which does not die. At the beginning of the session the dervish wears a black robe which he removes at the time of the dance, meaning that he is abandoning his gross individuality in order to appear purified before the master of the dance and before his brothers; the white robe in which he then dresses signifies the shroud in which his corpse will one day be wrapped and at the same time prefigures the resurrection and the joyous meeting with the Divine Beloved. During the session the dervish sings: "The frock is my tomb, the hat my tombstone…. Why wouldn't a corpse dance in this world when the sound of the trumpets raise the dead to dance?"

In their orchestra the Mawlawīs use the small violin with three strings, the lute, and above all the drum and the reed flute (*nay*) as their principal instruments. The reed flute is their favorite instrument and their most eloquent means of expression. The reed from which it is made is the symbol of human existence, fragile, fragmentary, since it is cut off from its origin just as the reed was pulled from the reed-bed.

266. Whirling dervishes

However, this existence can be regenerated when it is traversed and transformed by the divine Breath and is lent its strength, its energy, its voice.[29] In the prologue to the *Mathnawī* (*Mesnevi*), his mystical epic in 26,000 couplets, Rumi likens the song of the flute to the call of the soul which longs to return to his Lord: "Listen to the song of the reed and listen to its story. Weeping from the pain of separation it cries: 'Since I was severed from my native land, men and women have longed to hear my songs. And the agony of separation has broken my heart….'"[30]

One of the dominant themes of Mawlawī spirituality is that earthly music is an echo of celestial music. Harmonious vibration of strings, the repeated striking of the drum, the voice of the flute, are reminders of our divine origin and awaken in us the desire to find once again our distant homeland. The Koran (7: 172) teaches that in the beginning God made a solemn pact, with souls before creation, asking them "Am I not your Lord?" "Yea!", they responded, thus accepting perpetual obedience. Nevertheless, souls were unfaithful to the pact; they desired to live a separate existence which is the cause of all their miseries. To find again the original purity is therefore the most profound, the most normal aspiration of the human being. As a Mawlawī friend, a professor of French at the high school of Konya, who had just cited in the text the first verses of the "Lake" by Lamartine, once told me: "Each beautiful thing, a flower, the song of a bird, awakens in our soul the memory of our origin. Let us learn how to listen to the voice of beautiful things; it will make us understand the voice of our soul."

267. *Above*: Shrine and *tekke* (convent of the whirling dervishes) of Jalāl ad-Dīn Rūmī, Konya, Turkey

268. *Below*: Jalāl ad-Dīn Rūmī's tomb, Konya, Turkey

29. Cf. with a letter in which a dervish likens the *nay* to the "perfect man", cited by F. Meyerovitch, *Mystique et poésie en Islam—Rumi et l'ordre des Derviches tourneurs* (Paris: Desclée de Brouwer, 1972), 89.

30. Paraphrased from the *Traité sur la séance mawlawie* de Dīvāne Mehmed Tchelebi (16th century); cited in M. Molé, *Les Danses sacrées*, 248-249.

The dance itself, in the form which was inspired to Rūmī and which he transmitted to his disciples, draws its efficacy from a rich and eloquent symbolism as well as from its centering and focusing action upon the human faculties. Gathered into an octagonal enclosure, the dervishes arrange themselves to dance in several concentric orbits creating an image of the planets in the heavens. One dervish, usually the oldest, occupies the center of the room where he represents the "pole". He turns slowly in place, while the others, arranged in a crown shape, spin around and at the same time revolve about the orbits on which they were placed. The dance is accompanied by several gestures of the arms. At the beginning, the hands are crossed over the chest in a gesture of humility and contraction of the soul. Then the arms spread apart in a sign of expansion; the right hand opens towards the sky and the left hand turns towards the ground. By this gesture, the dervish indicates that he is opening himself to the grace of Heaven in a gesture of confidence and that he leads the grace thus received towards the terrestrial world and all the beings who inhabit it. Having become like a rotating cross, he moves about smoothly, his head slightly bowed, his shoulders held constantly at the same level. His white robe, swollen like a corolla, is the image of the fullness of the universe penetrated by Divine Wisdom, while the vertical axis of his body, elongated by the high tarboosh, is the sign of the exaltation to which the creature can accede only after his extinction in the All-Powerful.

Reproducing on earth the movements of the stars, themselves symbols of angelic powers and hierarchies, the dervish is conscious of participating in the universal harmony and of contributing to making the order that is in the skies reign here below. Giving himself up to the rhythm of celestial harmonies, he becomes an instrument through which divine Love communicates with creatures suffering from separation and from the cosmic illusion. Through his rotation, he affirms the unique Presence of God in all directions in space—"Wherever you turn, there is the Face of God" (Koran 2: 115)—and he identifies himself with this Center and omnipresent Principle.

4—SPIRITUAL PROGRESS

Whatever their operative strength, the collective rites alone could not assure arrival at the final steps of the journey towards God. Spiritual realization can only be an affair of each instant as is well put in the expression "son of the moment" by which the Sufi is defined. For each moment of the life of the disciple there is a corresponding *adab*, an etiquette, which can be a ritual practice, a correct behavior, or better still, an inner attitude in conformity with that which God expects from His servant. In fact, according to a teaching of Abū'l-'Abbās al-Mursī (d. 686/1287), who was the master of Ibn 'Atā'Allāh of Alexandria, "For the servant four moments exist, not one more: the blessing and

269-271. The *samā'* of the whirling dervishes

272. Shaykh Mohammad; he was a *faqīr* of the *malāmati* type, hiding his high spiritual degree with rather eccentric behavior

31. Cited by Ibn ʿAjībah in *Iqāz al-himana fī sharh al-Hikam* (Cairo: Mustafaʾl Babi al-Halabī, 1381/1961), 357.

32. See the commentary on this *hadīth* by "the greatest of shaykhs", Muhyi al-Dīn Ibn ʿArabī, taken from the "Treatise on Existence" (*Risālat al-wujūdiyya*) and entitled *Kitāb al-ajwiba* or *Kitāb al-alif*, trans. by T.H. Weir (London: Beshara Publications, 1976).

33. Ibn ʿAjībah, *Miʿrāj, al-muhāsaba waʾ l-mushārata* (rubrics 14-15); trans. J.-L. Michon, *Le Soufi marocain*, 190-191.

34. The *muhāsaba* found a famous exponent in the person of the Sufi Hārith Ibn Asad al-Muhāsibī (d. 243/857 in Kufah) who took his surname from it; on whom see M. Smith, *An Early Mystic of Baghdad* (London, 1935), Mahmoud Abdel-Halim, *Al-Muhasibi* (Paris: Geuthner, 1940), and J. Van Ess, *Die Gedankenwelt des Harits al-Muhasibi* (Bonn: Selbst Verlag des Orientalischen Seminar des Universit at Bonn, 1961).

the trial of which he is the object on the part of God, the obedience and the disobedience which he himself manifests. And at each of these moments, God has a right over his servant: in blessing, this right is gratitude; in trial constancy; in obedience, the awareness of grace; and in disobedience, repentance and contrition."[31]

In order to reach such a "presence of spirit" which allows, according to an expression frequently encountered in treatises on Sufism, "to render to each one and to each thing his due", the *faqīr* must follow, under the direction of his master, a discipline which includes two inseparable aspects: a sustained effort toward self-knowledge and daily spiritual exercises based essentially on invocation.

"Know Thyself"

That self-knowledge is not only the condition but the very goal of the mystical quest is affirmed by the *hadīth* of the Prophet, "He who knows himself knows his Lord".[32] Such a knowledge obviously would not stop at the simply psychological level, seeing that the human soul, the psyche, always makes up a fragmentary entity which veils the vision of the total Reality, of the Divine Self. However, the very existence of this veil allows on its own level for a seizure of the Source of existence, and the concern of the *faqīr* must be to render the veil transparent so that the lights of Heaven can illumine it and pass through it unhindered. This means first to recognize our shortcomings which are displeasing to God, that is, which prevent Him from shining in us, and to work toward their elimination through ascetic discipline. This is the purgative aspect of inner knowledge, the aspect which often predominates during the initial portion of the path. As for the positive aspect of this same knowledge, it consists in recognizing in oneself the reflection of the qualities and beauties of the Creator and of attributing to Him all glory, thus increasing the intimacy between the praiser and the Praised.

The practices recommended by the masters for better self-knowledge include notably the "setting of conditions" which takes place in the morning upon awakening and consists in admonishing oneself and in reaffirming one's intention to consecrate oneself entirely to God. One then tells oneself, "Here is a new day which will be a test for you, so force yourself, oh my soul, to fill each instant with that which draws you nearer to God...."[33] The same evening, the *faqīr* must proceed to a self-examination (*muhāsaba*, literally an accounting), the object of which is not only the assessment of how the morning's resolutions were followed, but a "gathering up of time" by evoking simultaneously the acts and the thoughts of the day in imitation of the man on the threshold of death who sees his entire life pass before him.[34]

The two operations are, in fact, only particular methods for maintaining a constant vigilance which the disciple must have in order not to waste time, not to be distracted by "that which does not concern him" and in order to keep himself constantly attentive to the desire of the Beloved. This vigilance is called *murāqaba*, a word derived from the Divine Name *al-Raqīb*, the All-Seeing, and it is synonymous with "the guarding of the heart". It is this same disposition of the soul that the Hesychasts, the recluses of the Eastern Orthodox Christian Church, described as "the way of all the virtues and all the commandments of God, which consists of tranquillity of the heart and of a mind perfectly free from all imagination".[35] If its importance has been stressed by such eminent masters as Muhāsibī, Qushayrī, and Ibn ʿAtāʾ Allāh al-Iskandarī,[36] it is for reasons identical to those of the Christian mystics who were adepts in the "prayer of the heart", the reason being that only an inner soul free from distractions and random thoughts can be illuminated by perpetual prayer.

The acquisition of *murāqaba* is the highest level of self-mastery, the victory on three fronts of the interior battle waged by the *faqīr*: that of the external faculties, which implies scrupulous respect to the legal prescriptions and abstentions; that of the internal faculties, where the battle consists of dispelling evil thoughts and of remaining fixed on the divine Presence; and that of the depths of the heart, in which no other concern must enter except that of the Adored. "Vigilance", wrote Ibn ʿAjībah, "is the source of all goodness and contemplation is in proportion to it; he whose vigilance is great will attain great contemplation."[37]

∽ *Perpetual Orison*

Whereas the exercises of introspection aim at purifying the human recipient and at making *faqr*, the blessed destitution, reign therein, the *dhikr*, the pronouncing of the Divine Word, is made to communicate to the *faqīr* His inexhaustible richness.

In accordance with the Koranic injunction to multiply the acts of invocation, each *tarīqah* suggests to its members, according to their level of preparation and their individual zeal, a large range of ejaculatory prayers. First comes the *wird* particular to the order, the same one that is sung in the collective sessions as we have seen earlier, and which each *faqīr* must recite twice a day, morning and night, using his rosary (*subhah*). The *shaykh* can, in addition, propose that the disciple regularly read certain litanies composed by the inspired masters, often by the founder of the *tarīqah*. These are, for example, among the Qādiriyyah the *Qunūt*, made up entirely of Koranic verses; among the Shādhiliyyah the *hizb al-bahr* and the *hizb al-barr* ("Incantations of the Sea and the Land") of the Imām Shādhilī or the *salāt mashishiyyah* by the "Pole" (ʿAbd al-Salām Ibn Mashīsh [d. 625/1228]), master of the former; among the Khalwatiyyah the *Wird al-Sattār*; among the Tijaniyyah the *Jawharat al-kamāl*, etc.[38]

Strictly speaking, however, the invocatory practices are those which are based on the systematic repetition of short formulas containing one or more Divine Names and, more particularly, of the *shahādah*, of the sole name *Allāh*, or of its substitute, the pronoun *Huwa*, He. Being acts of pure devotion performed in order to bring the *faqīr* face to face with

273. Al-Hajj Muhammad Boushāra, a dignitary of the Darqāwī Order, founded by Mulay al-ʿArabī ad-Darqāwī

35. According to Hesychius de Batos, cited in *La Philocalie*, trans. J. Gouillard (Paris, 1953), 202.

36. See P. Nwyia, *Ibn ʿAtāʾ Allāh (m. 709/1309) et la naissance de la confrérie shādhilite*; *hikma* no. 22, 96 and note at pages 242-243 (Beirut: Dar el-Machreq, 1972).

37. *Miʿrāj, al-murāqaba* (rubric 13); trans. J.-L. Michon, *Le Soufi marocain*, 189-190.

38. Many of these litanies, although composed originally by Sufis, later fell into the public domain and nourished popular piety, such as the *Dalāʾil al-khayrāt* of the Moroccan Imām Ibn Sulaymān al-Jazūlī (d. 870/1465), the *Hisn al-hasin* of Ibn al-Jazarī (d. 833/1429) and many others, a fairly complete repertory of which was compiled by C.E. Padwick, *Muslim Devotions* (London: S.P.C.K., 1961).

himself, to test his ability to offer the sacrifice of his thoughts and his feelings and to aid him in abandoning himself in God, these exercises require recollection and solitude. Thus, the invocation performed in retreat (*khalwah*) is the most often recommended mode of *dhikr*, the same one which the Prophet taught to 'Alī ibn Abī Tālib, his cousin and son-in-law. 'Alī, having once inquired about the shortest way to God, the Prophet answered, "'Alī, always repeat the Name of God in solitary places...." After this, with eyes closed, he said out loud three times, "*lā ilāha illā 'Llāh*", making 'Alī repeat this formula with the same intonation.[39] 'Alī later initiated Hasan al-Basrī to this *dhikr*, which has been perpetuated in numerous *turuq* such as the Khalwatiyyah, founded by the Persian anchorite 'Umar al-Khalwatī (d. in Cesaria, Syria in 800/1397). It should be noted that this *tarīqah*, always active in North Africa and the Near East, added to the invocation of the *shahādah* and the name *Allāh*, the pronoun *Huwa* and the four divine names *Haqq* (Truth), *Hayy* (Living), *Qayyūm* (Eternal), and *Qahhār* (Dominant). These seven names correspond to the celestial spheres, to the colors emanated by the fundamental Light, and to the stages of the soul on the path to perfection, the soul being first "prone to evil", then "blameworthy", "inspired", "appeased", "satisfied", "satisfying", before being rendered "perfect".[40]

A very similar teaching is found in the Suhrawardiyyah Order whose founder, Shihāb al-Dīn 'Umar, already mentioned concerning his advice on good companionship, also figures among the ancestors of the initiatic chain of the Khalwatīs. The Suhrawardī *dhikr* also includes seven names of which only the last two, *al-Rahmān* (the Merciful) and *al-Rahīm* (the Forgiving) differ from the preceding list. It is also practiced during retreats whose normal duration is forty days and is accompanied by the visualization of the seven symbolic colors: blue, yellow, red, white, green, black, and undifferentiated, which correspond to the various levels or worlds of universal manifestation.[41]

Of all the formulas of invocation, it is the name *Allāh* which, even among the *turuq* with a multiform *dhikr*, has always been considered as the most complete and the most efficacious way to grace. Thus it is, for example, that when the celebrated theologian Abū Hāmid al-Ghazzālī, after having exhausted the possibilities of speculative reasoning, had the desire to follow the path of direct experience and revealed this to a Sufi, he was given the following advice:

> The best method consists of breaking totally your ties with the world, in such a way that your heart is occupied with neither family nor ... money.... In addition you must be alone in a retreat to carry out, from among your acts of worship, only the prescribed *salāt* ... and, being seated, concentrate your thoughts on God, without other interior preoccupation. You will do this, first by saying the name of God with your tongue, repeating without ceasing *Allāh, Allāh*, without relaxing your attention.

274. Indication of the Brotherhoods
(*bayān at-turuq*)

39. Tradition reported by Sidi Yusuf al-'Ajamī in his work entitled *Rihān al-qulūb*; cited by H. Depont and O. Coppolani, *Les Confréries religieuses musulmanes* (Algiers: Jourdan, 1897), 370-372.

40. The Khalwatī teaching is recorded, particularly, in the *Fahrasa* (Book of Supports) of Si Muhammad b. Alī b. Sanūsī (d. 1276/1869) founder of the Sanūsiyyah *tarīqah* whose politico-religious authority rapidly spread to Tripolitania, Cyrenaica, and the Sudan. See L. Rinn, *Marabouts et Khouans* (Algiers: Jourdan, 1884), 295-299 and the table of the seven degrees leading to perfection, 300-301.

41. See *Kitāb 'Awārif al-ma'ārif* (Cairo: Maktaba 'Alawiya, 1358/1939), especially chaps. 26-28 which treat the merits and the modalities of this retreat called *arba'iniyya* (the "quarantine").

The result will be a state in which you will effortlessly feel this name in the spontaneous movement of your tongue.[42]

This is found as the first step in a process of inner penetration in three stages as suggested by the same Ghazzālī in his celebrated "Revival of the Sciences of Religion":

After seating himself in solitude, he (the *Sūfī*) does not cease to say with his mouth *Allāh, Allāh,* continually and with presence of heart. And he continues thus until he reaches a state wherein he abandons the movement of the tongue, and sees the word as if flowing upon the tongue. Then he arrives at the point of effacing any trace of the word upon his tongue, and he finds his heart continually applied to the *dhikr*; he perseveres assiduously, until he effaces from his heart the image of speaking, the letters and the shape of the word, and the meaning of the word alone remains in his heart, present in him, as if joined to him and not leaving him.[43]

275. Calligraphy of the Divine Name, *Allāh*

❧ *The Three Stages of Certainty*

In the same way that integral religion includes three stations capable of sanctifying the entire man, body, soul, and spirit, through submission (*islām*) to the prescriptions and prohibitions of the Law (*sharī'ah*), through the faith (*īmān*) which blooms on the spiritual path (*tarīqah*), and through the conformity (*iḥsān*) of the individual to the Divine Reality (*ḥaqīqah*), so the practice of the *dhikr*, which is the central method of this sanctification, takes place on three levels, that of deeds, that of qualities, and that of the Essence, and in each of these, achieves sanctifying union. In effect what occurs is the following:

1. the invocation of the tongue unites all the separate moments of the man in the single act of the *dhikr* and thus restores paternity to the only real Agent, which is God;

2. the invocation of the heart causes the appearance of all the qualities of the universe in a single place, a blessed center, while attributing them to the only One who is worthy to be qualified by the most beautiful Names;

3. the invocation of the depth of the heart, of the "secret" (*dhikr al-sirr*) has neither point of departure nor end, nor distinct subject and object; thanks to a clear vision it affirms that nothing exists except the One who is the Name, the Named, and the Namer, in His Absolute and Unconditional Essence.

Mastery of the first stage of the *dhikr*, which corresponds to the acquisition of the "science of certainty", is largely dependent on the clarity of the mind, thus on the aptitude of the *faqīr* to meditate upon himself (Koran 30: 8) as well as upon "the creation of the heavens and the earth" (3: 191) and, in general, upon all the signs of God (10:

42. *Mizān al-'amal,* cited by A.G. Wensinck, *La Pensée de Ghazzālī,* 144.

43. *Iḥyā' 'ulūm al-dīn* (Cairo, 1352 H.), chap. III, 16-17, cited by G.D. Anawati, and L. Gardet, *Mystique musulmane* (Paris: Vrin, 1961), 277.

24). Not only does meditation aid in eliminating distractions and in maintaining a fixed attention on the *dhikr*, but it causes doubt and existential worry to cease and confirms the disciple in his vocation of seeking God.

The second stage, that of the heart, is also that of "the eye" or "the source of certainty". It implies an unfailing adherence of the will, a confidence that the *dhikr* fills all needs and that it leads to salvation. It is the stage of love of God, that of the man who resides in the "inward dimension, the domain of unity, synthesis, and permanence".[44]

As for the third stage of the *dhikr*, that of the "truth of certainty", it is a gift from Heaven, incommensurate with the effort of the thought and will that preceded it. The individual abandons himself to it. He is said to have "disappeared", to be absorbed by the One invoked, and "made one" with Him. He becomes then, through a direct vision, a perfect witness to the Truth. According to the testimony of one of those who arrived at this final stage, the "master of the circle" of the Sufis of Baghdad, Abu al-Qāsim al-Junayd (d. 298/911), "This, then, is the highest stage of realization of the Unity of God by the worshipper who maintains this unity having lost his individual self".[45]

EPILOGUE

Over seventy-five years ago, in 1931, a great scholar of Muslim mysticism, Émile Dermenghem, published, along with the French translation of the famous poem of Ibn al-Fārid on the Mystical Wine, a letter which a young Moroccan had written him.[46] This young man described gatherings of *dhikr*, of invocation, which he had attended several years earlier in a small mosque in Fez. The dervishes who participated in these gatherings belonged to the Shādhiliyyah Order and the correspondent concluded his letter with these words: "All that, alas, is only a memory. … Where are the fakirs of yesteryear? The old ones have passed away or become infirm. The young ones have become modernized and prefer to spend their time drinking aperitifs in cafés or strolling through the new city. The Orient, unfortunately, is losing its essence along with its charm. The divine Breath which exhaled the verses of Ibn al-Fārid no longer fills chests. Where will this lead?"

No doubt these observations are true, this sadness is legitimate. Inexorably, all people are adopting, with varying degrees of enthusiasm, a mode of life as well as of thought—since one does not engage the body without engaging the soul—diametrically opposed to the course of religion and *a fortiori* to the mystical path. The Prophet Muhammad, or perhaps his son-in-law 'Alī, once said, "Act for this present world as if you were going to live forever, and act for the other world as if you were going to die tomorrow". More and more modern man, whether of the West or the East, has the tendency to retain only the first part of this advice; he devotes all his energy to organizing his well-being

44. F. Schuon, *Dimensions of Islam*, chap. 9 (see above, note 3): "Earthly Concomitances of the Love of God": "The man who 'loves God' … is one who dwells in … the 'inward dimension' … the domain of unity, synthesis, and permanence."

45. Ali Hassan Abdel-Kader, *The Life, Personality and Writings of Al-Junayd* (London: Luzac, 1962), 57 (Arabic text), 178 (English translation).

46. See note 22 above.

here on earth, as if this world would last forever. By doing this he loses sight of the fact that the passage on earth is, in reality, only one step; he forgets that according to the teaching of Jesus, Seyyidnā 'Isā, honored as a major Prophet in Islam, "Man does not live by bread alone, but by all the words which come from the mouth of God"; or that, according to the teaching of the Koran (93: 4), "The other life, certainly, is better for you than this one".

However, let us not be totally pessimistic. Behind the picture we are currently given of the Orient divided, prey to the agony of difficult economic, social, and political organization, remain stable values, an authentic civilization. Men remain, again according to a Koranic saying, whom "their trade does not distract from the remembrance of God" (24: 37). If certain spiritual centers have disappeared, others, even beyond the classical borders of the *dār al-islām*, have taken up the refrain which has lasted more than thirteen centuries. Thus, the Muslim Orient has not failed in its traditional mission, that which generations of dervishes and Sufis have fulfilled: to pass from century to century the good news that there exists a path which leads to God, and to guide along this path the souls enraptured by a Truth which never dies.

276. Two angels; detail from the *Mi'rāj* (ascension) of the Prophet, from a manuscript of the *Khamseh* of Nizami, 16th century

ILLUSTRATIONS

Frontispiece: Tile work from the Friday Mosque of Yazd, Iran

1. Tile work from the Alhambra, Granada, Spain
2. Sidi Halaoui minaret, Tlemcen, Morocco
3. Carved calligraphy from the *mihrāb* of the Friday Mosque of Isfahan, Iran
4. Tile work detail from the Friday Mosque of Isfahan, Iran
5. Entrance from the central courtyard to the prayer room of the Qarawiyyin Mosque, Fez, Morocco
6. Jabal Nūr (Mount Hira), Mecca, Saudi Arabia
7. The Mosque of 'Alī in al-Khandaq, Medina, Saudi Arabia
8. Jabal Tūr, the sacred mountain near Mecca, Saudi Arabia
9. The oratory of Salman Farsi in al-Khandaq, Medina, Saudi Arabia
10. The oasis of Medina, Saudi Arabia
11. View of the city of Medina, Saudi Arabia
12. Side arcade of the Great Mosque of Kairouan, Tunisia
13. Courtyard *qibla* side of the Great Mosque of Kairouan, Tunisia
14. The Amr Mosque, Cairo, Egypt
15. The Great Mosque of Córdoba, Spain
16. Courtyard of the Mosque of Ibn Tulun, Cairo, Egypt
17. Iraqi miniature depicting the city of Medina, 16th century; Dublin, Chester Beatty Library
18. Page from a pilgrimage guide depicting the Ka'bah at Mecca, 1582
19. Pilgrims around the Ka'bah in Mecca, Saudi Arabia
20. Carved inscription of the name of Muhammad, Mausoleum of Sultan Oljaitu, Soltaniyah, Iran
21. Selected Koranic *sūrah*s copied by al-Hajj Ahmad Na'ili, Ottoman Empire, 1808
22. Pages from an Egyptian Koran; Rayhani script with *sūrah* headings in ornamental Eastern Kufic, 8th/14th century; Dublin, Chester Beatty Library, 1521, ff 1v-2r
23-24. Pages from a Maghrebi collection of *hadīth*, 1204; Fez, al-Qarawiyyin University
25. The Mosque of the Prophet in Medina, Saudi Arabia; view of *al-Rawdah*, the area next to the tomb of the Prophet
26. The two formulae of the "attestation of faith"; Turkish tile, 16th century
27. *The Epistles of the Sincere Brethren* (Rasā'il Ikhwān al-Safā'), detail in the right frontispiece, Baghdad, Iraq, 287; Istanbul, Library of the Suleymaniye Mosque, Esad Efendi 3638, f 3v
28. *Maqāmāt* (the Assemblies) *of al-Harīrī*: Abu Zaïd delivering a sermon at the Barga'id Mosque, Baghdad, Iraq, 1230; Paris, Bibliothèque Nationale, ms. arabe 5847
29. Tile work detail from the Darb-e Imam Mosque, Isfahan, Iran
30. Inscribed brick in Kufic script from Turkey
31. The double *shahādah*, the two formulae of the "attestation of faith"
32. Prayer hall and *mihrāb* of the Great Mosque of Kairouan, Tunisia
33. Planispheric astrolabe, Iran, 12th century
34. Compass to determine the direction to Mecca (*qiblah*), Iran, 19th century
35. *Mihrāb* and *minbar* of the Sultan Hassan Mosque, Cairo, Egypt
36. Prayer hall of the Suleymaniye Mosque, Istanbul, Turkey
37. Pilgrims praying in front of the Ka'bah, Mecca, Saudi Arabia
38. Praying in the Great Mosque of Kairouan, Tunisia
39. Praying in the Mosque of Paris, France
40. Praying in the Friday Mosque of Isfahan, Iran
41. Praying in the courtyard of the mud-brick Friday Mosque at Ibb, Yemen
42. Praying in nature, Sudan
43. Praying in the Friday Mosque of Delhi, India
44. Praying in nature, Afghanistan
45. A guardian praying in the courtyard of the Madrasa Ben 'Ananiya, Fez, Morocco
46. Ablution fountain of al-Muayyad Mosque, Cairo, Egypt
47. Ablution fountain, Morocco
48. Performing the ritual ablution before prayers, Pakistan
49. Ablution fountain of the Wazi Khan Mosque, Lahore, Pakistan
50. Ablution fountain of the Qarawiyyin Mosque, Fez, Morocco
51. Cupola of the Tairuzi *hammām* in Damascus, Syria
52. Fountain of al-'Attarin, Fez, Morocco
53. Ablution fountain of the Mahabat Khan Mosque, Pakistan
54. Prayer hall of the Qarawiyyin Mosque, Fez, Morocco
55. *Mihrāb* and *minbar* of the Aqsunghur Mosque, Cairo, Egypt
56. Shah Mosque, Lahore, Pakistan
57. Jame (Friday) Mosque, Isfahan, Iran
58. Al-Bourdeni Mosque, Cairo, Egypt
59. Koranic teaching at the al-Azhar Mosque, Cairo, Egypt
60. The dome treasury (*bayt al-māl*) in the courtyard of the great Umayyad Mosque, Damascus, Syria
61. *A Muslim Giving Alms*, Bustan of Sadi, Bihza, Persian miniature, 15th century; Cairo, National Library of Egypt
62. The door of the Ka'bah
63. The Ka'bah, Mecca, Saudi Arabia
64. Jabal Rahmah (Mount of Mercy), Arafat, Saudi Arabia
65. Pilgrim tents in Arafat, Saudi Arabia
66. Pilgrims performing *sa'ai* (seven rounds in a defined mode) between the hilltops Safah and Marwah
67. Pilgrims waiting for the sunset on Jabal Rahmah, Arafat, Saudi Arabia
68. The main entrance to the Mosque of Mecca, Saudi Arabia
69. The Prophet's Mosque, Medina, Saudi Arabia
70. The Kutubiyyah Mosque, Marrakesh, Morocco
71. The Zaytuna Mosque and University, Tunis, Tunisia
72. Kasbah of Ait Banhaddou, High Atlas, Morocco
73. The Bab Mellah, Fez, Morocco
74. The minaret of al-Siba'iyya Madrasa, Damascus, Syria
75. The Gök Madrasa, Turkey
76. The Tilla Kari Madrasa, Samarkand, Uzbekistan
77. Prayer hall of the Qarawiyyin Mosque, Fez, Morocco
78. Courtyard of the Mustansiriya Madrasa, Baghdad, Iraq
79. The door of the Ince Minara Madrasa, Konya, Turkey
80. Chahar Bagh Madrasa, Isfahan, Iran
81. Char Minar, entrance to the Khalif Niyazkul Madrasa, Bukhara, Uzbekistan
82. Al-'Attarin Madrasa, Fez, Morocco
83. The Shirda Madrasa, Samarkand, Uzbekistan
84. Courtyard of al-Azhar Mosque and University, Cairo, Egypt
85. A muslim school in Indonesia
86. Tuareg tent set up for a Koranic reading, Niger
87. Koranic school of the Ifentar tribe in Tassila, south Morocco
88. A child learning to read the Koran, Niger
89. Tile work from the *mihrāb* of the Wazi Khan Mosque, Lahore, Pakistan
90. Inscription on the facade of the Bibi Khanum Mosque, Samarkand, Uzbekistan
91. Tile work detail from Morocco
92. The Generalife Gardens, Alhambra, Granada, Spain
93. The Shah Mosque, Isfahan, Iran
94. Ksar Goulmina, a fortress in Morocco
95. The Aljafería Palace, Zaragoza, Spain
96. Koran illuminated by 'Abd Allāh ibn Muhammad al-Hamadānī for the Sultan Ülljaytū, Hamadan, Iran; frontispiece to part 28, ff. 1v-2r; Cairo, National Library of Egypt
97. Anonymous single-volume Koran, Ottoman Empire, c. 1750-1800
98. The Suleymaniye Mosque, Istanbul, Turkey

99. Koran 13: 28: "Verily in the remembrance of *Allāh* do hearts find rest"; calligraphy by Shahriar Piroozram
100. A calligrapher in Tunis, Tunisia
101. *Hadīth*: "Verily God is beautiful; He loves beauty"; calligraphy by Shahriar Piroozram
102. Detail of a *kiswah* (embroidered black cloth which covers the Ka'bah)
103. Qutub Minar, Delhi, India
104. Brass lamp from Isfahan, Iran
105. Engraved washbowl from the Timurid period, Iran
106. Tannery in the old quarter of Fez, Morocco
107. The Fondouk Sagha, built in 1749-50, Fez, Morocco
108. Mosaic from the Great Mosque of Damascus, Syria
109. Mosaics from the Great Mosque of Córdoba, Spain
110. Brick inscription, Friday Mosque, Isfahan, Iran
111. Wall decoration in glazed earthenware (*zellij*), Fez, Morocco
112. Earthenware mosaic, Chah-i-Zindeh, Samarkand, Uzbekistan
113. Page from an Eastern Kufic Koran, Koufa, Iraq, 11th century; Rabat, Bibliothèque général et archives du Maroc
114. Page from a Maghrebi Koran, 13th century
115. Frontispiece of an illuminated Koran, Egypt, 14th century; Richard Ettinghausen, *Arab Painting* (Lausanne, 1962)
116. Tile work from the Alhambra, Granada, Spain
117. Tile work on the ceiling of the Chahar Bhag Madrasa, Isfahan, Iran
118. View of the city of Baghdad, Iraq
119. View of the city of Yazd, Iran
120. View of the city of Damascus and its *ghuta* (oasis), Syria
121. The Khaju Bridge in Isfahan, Iran
122. Ahuan caravanserai, Semnan, Iran
123. Bab Dakakine, Fez, Morocco
124. The inner city of Khiva, encircled by crenellated walls, Uzbekistan
125. Aerial view of the Friday Mosque, Isfahan, Iran
126. Traditional architecture in the city of Sana'a, Yemen
127. The city of Moulay Idriss Zerhoun, Morocco
128. A *ksar* (fortified village) in the Draa Valley, south Morocco
129. Aerial view of a village in the Tafilalet, south Morocco
130. Aerial view of Marrakesh, Morocco
131. Courtyard of the Prophet's Mosque, Medina, Saudi Arabia
132. *Mihrāb* of the Prophet's Mosque, Medina, Saudi Arabia
133. The Great Mosque of Dakar, Senegal
134. The *mihrāb* of the Great Mosque of Kairouan, Tunisia
135. The *minbar* of the Sokullu Mosque in Istanbul, Turkey
136. Mosque-Madrasa of Registan square, Samarkand, Uzbekistan
137. The Taj Mahal, Agra, India
138. Mausoleum of Farīd ad-Dīn 'Attar, Neishabour, Iran
139. The Hatters market (Tcharsouk), Samarkand, Uzbekistan
140. One of the alleys of the bazaar of Isfahan, Iran
141. Stucco claustras of a house in Sana'a, Yemen
142. Wooden balconies in an old street of Mecca, Saudi Arabia
143. Tomb of Shaykh Ni'matullāh, Mahan, Iran
144. Detail from the hospital and mausoleum of Keykavus I, Sivas, Turkey
145. Tiled inscription on the dome of the Shaykh Lotfollah Mosque, Isfahan, Iran
146. Embroidered cloth covering the door to the Ka'bah
147. Tiled inscription from the Tuman Akha Mosque, Samarkand, Uzbekistan
148. Panel with carved inscription, Egypt
149. Kufic calligraphy, Herat, Afghanistan
150. Contemporary plate from Kutahya, Turkey
151. Page from a North-African Koran in Maghrebi script, 1304; Munich, Bayerische Staatsbibliothek
152. Page from an Eastern Kufic Koran, Iraq, Persia, or Afghanistan, 1092; Tehran, collection of the late Āqā Mahdī Kāshānī

153. Ornamental page from a Persian Koran, 19th century; private collection
154. Page from a Koran in Muhaqqaq script with *sūrah* headings in ornamental Kufic script, Cairo, Egypt, 1320-1330; Cairo, National Library of Egypt
155. Tiled *mihrāb* of the Madrasa Imami, Isfahan, Iran
156. Floral decoration, Registan, Sher Dor Madrasa, Samarkand, Uzbekistan
157. *Zellij* from the Bahia Palace, Marrakesh, Morocco
158. Claustras around the courtyard of the al-'Attarin Madrasa in Fez, Morocco
159. Ceramic panel *mihrāb* reproducing *sūrah* 97, Kashan, Iran, 13th century
160. Mosque lamp from Egypt, bearing the inscription of the "Verse of Light"
161. Prayer rug with a niche design
162. The Dome of the Rock, Jerusalem, Palestine
163. Qaytbay Mausoleum, Cairo, Egypt
164. Gur-e Amir Mausoleum, Samarkand, Uzbekistan
165. Ceiling of the Shah Mosque, Isfahan, Iran
166. *Muqarnas* at the pavilion of the Court of Lions, Alhambra, Granada, Spain
167. Stucco decoration at the pavilion of the Court of Lions, Alhambra, Granada, Spain
168-169. Carved plaster panels (left) and brick *muqarnas* (right) of the Abbasid Palace, Baghdad, Iraq
170. Lattice at the Taj Mahal, Agra, India
171. Mausoleum of Akbar, Sikandra, India
172. Berber wooden grid in a kasbah (fortress) in Agadir, Morocco
173. Wooden lattice in the Mosque of al-Hakim, Isfahan, Iran
174. A courtyard of a house in Córdoba, Spain
175. The fountain of the Court of Lions, Alhambra, Granada, Spain
176. Irrigation at Kerzaz, Algeria
177. Water wheel on the Orontes River, Hama, Syria
178. The Fin Gardens, Kashan, Iran
179. The Generalife Gardens, Alhambra, Granada, Spain
180. The Bagh-e Faiz Baksh, Shalimar Gardens, Lahore, Pakistan
181. *Rustam with His Mistress in a Garden Pavilion*, Mughal miniature, 15th century
182. Mughal miniature showing the garden of Bagh-e Vafa, near Kabul, Afghanistan, 1508
183. The Generalife Gardens, Alhambra, Granada, Spain
184. Palais Jamai, Fez, Morocco
185. *Horsemen Waiting to Participate in a Parade*; from the *Maqāmāt of al-Harīrī*, Baghdad, Iraq, 13th century; Paris, Bibliothèque Nationale, ms. Arabe 5847
186. *Youth Reading*, Mughal miniature, Deccani School, India, c. 1610
187. Mughal miniature, 18th century
188. Safavid miniature, 16th century
189. *The Prophet and the Angel*, Safavid miniature, 16th century; Geneva, Musée d'Art et d'Histoire
190. Floor carpet detail, Uzbekistan
191. Bokhara *ensi* carpet
192. Tent and loom of the Bedouin Bani Na'imāt, south Jordan
193. Folk Festival in the Berber Zemmour tribe (Khemisset Province), Morocco
194. "Kuwaiti chest" produced in the Gulf area
195. Painted chest of the Jbaala country, in the vicinity of Tangiers, Morocco
196. Carpet from Moroccan High Atlas area
197. Basket weaver, Salalah, Oman
198. Coppersmith shop, bazaar in Isfahan, Iran
199. Silversmith, Buramy, Oman
200. Traditional embroidery, Morocco
201. Coppersmith in Isfahan, Iran

202. Weavers in Morocco
203. Silversmith in Isfahan, Iran
204. A potter in Morocco
205. Weaver in the village of Harrania, close to the Pyramids, Egypt
206. Embroidery workshop, Rabat, Morocco
207. Potter in the Coptic neighborhood of Cairo, Egypt
208. Qashqais carpet weaver, Iran
209. Carpet from Kerman, Iran
210. *Joseph Listening to Music*, from the manuscript *Yusuf and Zulaykha* by Jāmī, Tabriz, Iran, 1540; Dublin, Chester Beatty Library
211. Drums, tambourines, and flutes
212. Detail from a Persian miniature, late 16th century; Boston, Museum of Fine Arts
213. Detail from a Persian miniature, Timurid dynasty, 1425-50; Boston, Museum of Fine Arts
214. Mawlawī dervishes
215. Members of a brotherhood playing the *daira*, Sanandaj, Iran
216. Member of a brotherhood using the *darabuka* in religious music, Fez, Morocco
217. Player of the double *nay*
218. Members of a Moroccan Sufi brotherhood
219. An Arab playing the "monochord", Yemen
220. Lute (*'ūd*)
221. Dombak goblet drum, Iran
222. *Rabāb* (rebec)
223. Ceramic drums
224. Drum player from Central Asia
225. Tar player from Central Asia
226. Traditional Berber dancers from the High Atlas, Morocco
227. Turkish miniature depicting Bilāl, the first muezzin, calling the faithful to prayer from the Ka'bah in Mecca, Saudi Arabia
228. Call to prayer from a mosque in Iran
229. The whirling dervishes in Konya, Turkey
230-231. Musicians from Iran
232-233. *Qawwālī* in progress at the shrine of Nizām al-Dīn, New Delhi, India
234. *Tanbūr*
235. Detail from a Persian manuscript
236. *Story of Bayād and Riyād; Bayād Singing and Playing the 'Ūd before the Lady and her Handmaidens.* Spain or Morocco, 13th century; Vatican, Biblioteca Apostolica, ms. Ar. 368 f 10r
237. Folk music performance from Morocco
238. Dancers and musicians of the Gnawa brotherhood, Tangiers, Morocco
239. *Kamāncheh*
240. Persian miniature depicting a drinking session in which wine and music lead to ecstatic rapture
241. A Mawlawī dervish playing the flute
242. Detail from a Mughal miniature, Lucknow, India, 18th century

243. Musicians in Tangiers, Morocco
244. A woman from Tiznit playing the *rabāb*, Morocco
245. Page from an illuminated Koran
246. Frontispiece from a Maghrebi Koran, Spain, 13th century; Istanbul, Topkapi Palace Museum Library, E.H. 219, f 1v
247. Praying at the Qarawiyyin Mosque, Fez, Morocco
248. Sidi Ahmed from Meknes, belonged to the category of "wandering dervishes"
249. A member of the Naqshabandiyya Order guards the tomb of Qusam Ibn Abbas, cousin of the Prophet Muhammad, in Shah-i Zindeh, Samarkand, Uzbekistan
250. A pilgrim in Morocco
251. Members of the Harrāqiyya Order, a Moroccan Sufi brotherhood
252. A dervish from the Mawlawī Order reading Rūmī's *Mathnawi*
253. A Sufi master of the 20th century, Shaykh Muhammad al-Hāshimī
254. Shaykh Mulay 'Alī al-Darqāwī
255. Shaykh Ahmad ibn Mustafa al-'Alawī, founder of the Darqāwiyyah-'Alawiyyah Order, a branch of the Shādhiliyyah Order
256. Members of the Tijaniyya Order at the mausoleum of Sidi Ahmad Tijani, Fez, Morocco
257. *Dhikr* session in Baghdad, Iraq
258. The ninety-nine Names of *Allāh*
259. *Hadīth*: "There is a way of polishing everything and removing rust and that which polishes the heart is the invocation of God"; calligraphy by Muhammad Zachariah
260. The Divine Name, *Allāh*
261. "There is no god but God" (*Lā ilāha illā 'Llāh*); calligraphy by Khurshid Alam
262. *Dhikr* session in Aleppo, Syria
263. *Dervishes Dancing*, miniature from the *Khamsah* of Amir Khusrau, 1485
264. Detail from an illustration to Rūmī's *Mathnawi*, Herat, Afghanistan, 1458-1459; Washington, D.C., Vever Collection, Smithsonian Institution
265. A bandir player, participating in a *dhikr* session of a Sufi brotherhood in Meknes, Morocco
266. Whirling dervishes
267. Shrine and *tekke* of Jalāl ad-Dīn Rūmī, Konya, Turkey
268. Jalāl ad-Dīn Rūmī's tomb, Konya, Turkey
269-271. The *samā'* of the whirling dervishes
272. Shaykh Mohammad, a *faqīr* of the *malāmatī* type
273. Al-Hajj Muhammad Boushāra, a dignatary of the Darqāwī Order
274. Indication of the Brotherhoods (*bayān at-turuq*)
275. Calligraphy of the Divine Name, *Allāh*
276. Detail from the *Mi'rāj* (ascension) of the Prophet, from a manuscript of the *Khamseh* of Nizami, 16th century; London, British Library, Or. 2265, f.1958

PHOTO CREDITS

INDEX

Abbasid Caliphate, 15, 54, 95n, 104
'Abd al-Ghanī al-Nābulusī, 137, 138n
Abd al-Qādir al-Jīlānī, 128, 136
'Abd al-Rahmān II, 112
ablution, 21, 63, 77
Abraham, 20, 28, 29, 80
Absolute Being, 10, 100, 135
Abū Bakr, 12, 13, 125, 126, 139
Abū'l-Dardā', 135
Abū Hanifah, 14
Abū Hurayrah, 125
adab, 143
adhān, 105
ahellel, 118
Āhl-i-Haqq ("People of the Truth"), 107, 109
Akbar, Emperor, 117
al-'Alawī, Ahmad, 86
alchemy, 43, 97; of light, 76; of the Word, 57
'Alī ibn Abī Talīb, 13, 15, 108, 125, 146, 148.
    See also Lion of God
Almería, 6
alms-giving (*zakāt*), 16, 17, 25, 26, 27, 62, 129,
    134, 135; *zakāt al-fitr*, 26
Amīr Khusraw, 108, 117
Andalusia, 112, 129
arabesque, 52, 58, 71, 76, 116
artisans, 52, 53, 76, 84, 85, 95; Supreme
    Artisan, 76
Attributes (of God), 57, 127. *See also*
    Qualities
'azādārī, 107
Baghdad, 5, 42, 43n, 54, 82, 111, 124, 148
Balkh, 6
Baqlī, Rūzbihān, 113
barakah, 118, 128
Barzanjī, Shaykh, 106
Basrah, 5, 42, 43n, 56
Beauty, 57, 99, 108, 112, 119; of God, 51, 114
Bedouins, 4, 83
Bektāshī Order, 116
Berbers, 118; of North Africa, 54
bhava, 117
bid'ah (innovations), 15
Bilāl, 126
brotherhoods, 52, 86, 128, 129n, 133, 139,
    140; Sufi, 42, 57, 97, 109
Buddhism, 126
Bukhara, 6
Bukhārī, 12
Burckhardt, Titus, 58n, 62, 76, 133
Burdah, 106, 138
al-Būsīrī, Shaykh Muhammad, 106, 138
al-Būzīdī, Shaykh, 98
Byzantine, 8, 126; artists, 54; Christianity,
    126; empire, 5; law, 15
Cairo, 63, 72, 82. *See also* Fustāt
calamus, 50
Caliphate, 16, 33; of 'Umar, 5
calligraphy, 50, 55, 57, 57n, 67, 81, 104
carpet, 53, 58, 72, 84; symbolism of, 84
Chishtī, Mu'īn al-Dīn, 108, 117
Chishtī Order, 108, 117

Christianity, 28, 128
Civitas Romano, 4
Coptic Egypt, 54
Córdoba, 6, 54, 112
crafts, 53, 67, 85, 86, 87, 87n; craftsmanship,
    62, 86
Damascus, 6, 54, 60, 82
al-Daqqāq, Abu Alī, 136
dār al-Islām, 13, 33, 34, 91, 118, 149
al-Darqāwī, Mawlāy al-'Arabī, 98, 113
Darqāwiyya Order, 132, 139
dhikr, 11, 51, 62, 99, 129, 133, 135, 136, 140,
    141, 145, 146, 147, 148; *dhikr al-sadr*, 140
Dhū'l-Nun the Egyptian, 92
dhrupad, 117
esoterism, 16, 40, 109, 123, 134
Essence, the Divine, 56, 58, 76, 77, 96, 132,
    139, 147; Absolute, 138
Euclid, 92
exoterism, 134
faqīh, 25, 35
faqīr (pl. *fuqarā*'), 43, 97, 98, 124, 129, 133,
    136, 138, 139, 144, 145, 147
faqr, 102, 124, 125, 145
al-Fārābī, Abū Nasr, 94, 100, 104, 111
fasting, 16, 17, 20, 25, 26, 134; fast of
    Ramadan, 25, 42, 123
fatwā, 16, 35
Fedeli d'amore, 113
Fez, 6, 27, 62, 63, 82, 112, 148
fuqahā', 35, 37, 87
Fustāt (old Cairo), 5, 63
futuwwāt, 42
Gabriel (angel of Revelation), 25, 49, 109,
    123, 124, 125
gardens, 60, 61, 77, 79, 82, 107, 108, 112; of
    Eden, 45, 84
al-Ghazzālī, Abū Hāmid, 93n, 96, 98, 126,
    146, 147
Ghazzālī, Ahmad, 93n, 99, 100, 139
geometry, 58; sacred, 76
ghazal, 109, 110, 117
ghinā', 56, 103
gnosis, 95, 99, 106, 123n, 126, 136
Greece, 54, 94
guedra, 118
guilds, 42, 52, 53, 86
habūs, 26, 27
hadīth, 8, 12, 15, 20, 27, 40, 42, 51, 56, 91n,
    98, 144; of Gabriel, 44, 136; *qudsī*, 26, 77
hadrah, 138, 139, 140; *hadrat al-dhikr*, 138
Hāfiz, 110
hāfiz, 40
hajj, 28, 30
Hanbalite School, 14, 15
hanīf, 29, 80
Hanifite School, 14
haqīqah, 44, 137, 147
Hakki, Ismail, 110
al-Harrāq, Muhammad, 113
Harrāqiyyah Order, 113
Hellenism, 54, 55, 81, 110

Hesychasts, 145
Holy War (*jihād*), 5, 7, 8, 26, 32; *al-jihād
    al-akbar*, 128
Hujwīrī, 91n, 92, 97, 128
hurm, 60, 61
Huseyn, Imām, 107
Ibn Abī'l Dunyā, 93
Ibn 'Ajibah, 98, 136, 144 145,
Ibn 'Arabī, Muhyi al-Dīn, 44, 129, 144n
Ibn 'Atā' Allāh al-Iskandarī, 143, 145
Ibn Bājja (Avempace), 94
Ibn al-Fārid, 'Umar, 44, 110, 138n, 148
Ibn Hanbal, Ahmad 14, 93
Ibn Khurdādhbih, 95
Ibn al-Jawzī, 93
Ibn Mashīsh, 'Abd al-Salām, 145
Ibn Misjāh, 111
Ibn Sīnā (Avicenna), 44, 94, 95
Ibn Zaylah, 95
'Īd al-fitr, 26
'Īd al-Kabīr, 30
ihsān, 85, 123, 124, 132, 137, 147
ijmā', 8, 14, 15
ijtihād, 14, 16, 35
Ikhwān al-Safā', 59, 91, 94, 110
imām, 25, 61, 62, 63, 105
'imārah (sacred dance), 139
Imām Shādhilī, 128, 145
Imām Shāfi'ī, 14, 15
imān, 123, 137, 147
Immanence, 57, 99
Initiation, 128, 129, 130, 131, 136
al-*insān al-kāmil*, 105
Intellect, 50, 137
Iraq, 109, 138
'Īsā (Jesus), Seyyidnā, 149
'Īsāwiyyah Order, 139, 140
islām, 12, 123, 136, 147
Ismā'īlism, 16n, 109
itqān, 85
ittihād, 127
Ja'far Ibn Abī Tālib, 139
Jāmī, 110
jannah, 79. *See also* Paradise
Judaism, 28
al-Junayd, Abū al-Qāsim, 9, 148
Ka'bah, 6, 19, 28, 29, 30, 52, 62, 63, 66, 80
Kairouan, 5, 63
kamāncheh, 111, 116
al-Karkhī, Ma'ruf, 126
Kāshifī, Husayn Wā'iz, 107
khalwah, 146
al-Khalwatī, 'Umar, 146
Khalwatiyyah Order, 116, 145, 146
khayāl, 117
al-Kindī, Ya'qūb, 94, 95, 101, 112
kiswah, 66
knowledge, 35, 50, 53, 62, 105, 126; divine,
    144; self-, 97, 144; spiritual way of, 136
Koran, *passim*; school, 40; schools of reading,
    56n
Kufah, 5, 42, 43n

Law, 33, 62; divine, 3, 9, 10; Koranic, 25, 26, 32, 40, 86; of nature, 59; religious, 30, 34, 43, 51, 91, 127, 137, 147; Revealed, 16, 34, 35; schools of, 14
laylat al-Qadr, 25
Lion of God, 108. *See also* 'Alī ibn Abī Talīb
litanies, 57, 105, 119, 129, 145
love, 26, 96, 97, 104; divine, 44, 130, 141, 143; of the Absolute, 116; of God, 125, 148; of the Master, 130; spiritual way of, 138. See also *mahabbah*
macrocosm, 102
madhhab, 14
madrasa, 37, 63, 76
Maghreb, 42, 112, 118, 138, 140
mahabbah, 136, 138
al-Mahdī, Imām, 15, 16, 34
makhāfah, 136
Malik, Imām, 56. *See also* Malik Ibn Anas
Malik Ibn Anas, 14
Malikite School, 14
Mamluk period, 72
al-Mansur, Caliph, 5
maqām, 101, 102, 116
ma'rifah, 136
masalla, 25
mashrabiya, 66, 76
materia prima, 77
Mathnawī, 114, 142
mawladiyyāt, 57, 106
Mawlawī Order, 100, 104, 106, 108, 116, 138, 139, 140
al-Mawsilī, Ishāq, 95, 111, 112
Mazdeism, 126
Mecca, 6, 19, 21, 27, 28, 30, 52, 62, 63, 66, 72, 80, 93, 125
Medina, 6, 13, 32, 62, 63, 125
melodic modes, 101; Hindustani, 109; Kurdish, 109; Persian, 116
Mesopotamia, 54, 81
microcosm, 102, 104, 117
mihrāb, 19, 25, 54, 63, 66, 72, 84
minbar, 25, 63
morals, 12, 35, 41, 42, 57, 97
Moses, 96
Mount Hira, 125
muftī, 35
Mughal India, 76, 82, 117
Muharram, 107
Muhāsibī, 145
muhtasib, 41, 42
Mullā Sadrā, 44
muqarnas, 76
murābitun, 42
murāqaba, 145
murshid, 128, 130, 135
al-Mursī, Abū'l-'Abbās, 143
muwaqqit, 21
mysticism, 40, 44, 62, 105, 125, 126, 148
nafs, 97
Names (of God), 11, 43, 62, 127, 133, 134, 135, 138, 140, 141, 145, 146; the most beautiful Names, 11, 112, 134, 135, 147; of Majesty, 135; of the Essence, 139, 146; of Mercy, 146. *See also* Supreme Name

Nāsiriyyah Order, 139
Nasr, Seyyed Hossein, 10n, 16, 123, 130, 131
nawbah, 100, 112, 113, 118
nay, 100, 104, 116, 141
Near East, 81, 86, 104, 146
Nichomacus, 92
Nizām al-Dīn Awliyā', 108
Noah, 86
Ottoman Caliphate, 33
painting, 81; Arab, 81; Mughal, 82; Persian, 82
Paradise, 28, 77, 79, 96, 114, 141
Pax Islamica, 6
Persia, 54, 58, 110, 114
peşrev, 116
pīr, 97, 109, 128, 130
Pīr-Binyānūn, 109. *See also* Gabriel
Plato, Platonism, 34, 94
poetry, 93, 103, 110, 112, 118; Arabic, 58; Sufi, 108, 137
Primordial Covenant, 99, 118
Prophet (Muhammad), 3, 6, 7, 8, 10, 12, 13, 14, 15, 25, 26, 27, 28, 30, 32, 35, 40, 41, 49, 51, 52, 54, 55, 56, 57, 62, 63, 77, 80, 85, 87, 91, 97, 103, 104, 105, 106, 107, 108, 112, 123, 124, 125, 126, 128, 131, 134, 135, 136, 137, 138, 139, 144, 146, 148
psalmody (recitation), 56; Koranic, 50, 55, 56, 71, 104, 105, 139; schools of, 56n; Byzantine, 106
Ptolemy, 92
Pythagoras, 72, 92
Qādiriyyah Order, 128, 133, 136, 138, 140, 145
qanūn, 100, 111, 116
qawwāli, 108, 117
qiblah, 19, 25
qirā'a, 56
qissariyas, 65
qiyās, 14, 15
Qualities (divine), 12, 56, 57, 131, 135, 144
al-Qūmī, Abū Ya'qūb, 129
rabāb, 100, 111, 112
raga, 101
Ramadan, 25, 123
ramelmayā, 112
rasa, 117
rāy, 14, 15
al-Rāzī, Abū Bakr, 94
Reality, 126, 135, 137, 144, 147
Revelation, 49, 50, 51, 55, 67, 94, 97, 119, 123, 134
Rifā'iyyah Order, 140
Roman Empire, 54
Rūmī (Jalāl al-Dīn), 44, 106, 110, 114, 128, 130, 143
ryad, 79
sabr, 12
Sa'diyyah Order, 140
Safi al-Dīn, 94
salāt, 138
samā', 92, 93, 96, 97, 104, 108, 112, 114, 116, 117, 133, 137, 138, 139, 140, 141
Samarkand, 6, 87
sāni, 52

Sassanid Empire, 5, 54
Schuon, Frithjof, 51, 92n, 126, 135, 148
Shādhiliyyah Order, 106, 128, 133, 136, 138, 140, 145, 148
Shafi'ite School, 14
Shāh Nāmeh, 108
shahādah, 10, 16, 105, 123, 136, 145, 146
Shams al-Dīn Tabrīzī, 130
sharī'ah, 10, 14, 17, 33, 34, 35, 44, 51, 97, 127, 137, 147
shaykh, 97, 128, 129, 130, 131, 133, 136, 137, 140, 145
Shī'ite, 15, 16, 30, 107, 109, 114; Imāms, 15, 104, 107, 108; Twelve Imām Shī'ism, 15, 16, 34
Shinto, 139
shirk, 26
silsilah, 130, 136
Sufism, 57n, 86, 92, 98, 99, 107, 109, 123, 125, 126, 129, 131, 133, 137, 144
al-Suhrawardī, Shihāb al-Dīn 'Umar, 131
Suhrawardiyyah, Order 146
Sunnah, 3, 10, 12, 13, 14, 26, 27, 37, 43, 51, 91, 105, 125, 128, 134
Sunnite Islam, 14, 15, 16, 30, 33, 34, 35
Supreme Name, 67, 135
tajallī, 58, 76
tajwīd, 56
takbīr, 25
Tamerlane, 87
tanbūr, 100, 109
tarīqah, 42, 97, 101n, 128, 129, 133, 136, 137, 145, 146, 147
tartīl, 56
tasawwuf, 62, 126
Tijaniyyah Order, 145
al-Tirmīdhī, 12, 135
Transcendence, 10, 57
Tunis, 6, 118
'ūd, 111
'ulamā', 35, 40, 62, 87
'Umar, 12
ummah, 4, 51
'Uthmān, 12
Umayyad Caliphate, 33, 55, 110
Umayyad Dynasty, 14, 54, 81
Unity (divine), 3, 4, 10, 11, 12, 17, 29, 43, 55, 57, 62, 67, 123, 148; of Being, 76
Vacare Deo, 124
Visigoths, 54
waqf, 26, 27
whirling dervishes, 100, 106, 116, 130, 133, 138, 139, 140
wird, 136, 137, 138, 145
Yār, 109
Yūnus Emre, 110
Zarrūqiyya Order, 139
zāwiyah, 27, 40, 133, 137
Ziryāb, 112
zūrkhāneh, 107

BIOGRAPHICAL NOTES

JEAN-LOUIS MICHON is a traditionalist writer, editor, translator, Arabist, and artistic consultant. He was born in France in 1924. Following his high school and initial university studies, Michon's early interest in comparative religion and Islam took him to Damascus, Syria, where he taught high school from 1946 to 1949. While there, he studied Arabic and immersed himself in the beauty and harmony of Islamic civilization. Once back in Europe, he obtained a degree in architectural drafting in Lausanne, Switzerland in 1952. Around this time he began a long association with eminent thinkers of the school of "perennial philosophy", such as Frithjof Schuon and Titus Burckhardt.

After marriage and the birth of a daughter, he began a career with a variety of United Nations agencies, first as a freelance editor and translator and finally, over a period of 15 years (1957-1972), as a permanent senior translator for the World Health Organization in Geneva. These assignments gave him the chance to visit many countries, a number of which belong to *dār al-islām* ("the world of Islam").

It was also during this period that Michon obtained a Ph.D. in Islamic studies at Paris University (Sorbonne). His thesis was on the life and works of a scholar and spiritual guide of great renown from the north of Morocco, Shaykh Ahmad Ibn 'Ajībah al-Hasanī (1747-1809), whose "Autobiography" (*Fahrasa*) and *Glossary of Technical Terms of Sufism (Mi'raj al-tashawwuf ilā haqā'iq al-tasawwuf)* Michon translated from Arabic into French (Milan: Archè, 1982; Paris: Vrin, 1974 and 1990). Michon's French translation of the *Fahrasa* of Ibn 'Ajībah has been translated into English by David Streight (Louisville: Fons Vitae, 1999).

From 1972 to 1980, Dr. Michon was Chief Technical Adviser to a series of joint programs of UNESCO, the UN Development Programme, and the Moroccan government, to be carried out in Morocco. These programs were for the preservation of traditional arts and crafts, and included the establishment of a broad survey of cultural property, covering inventories of national monuments and sites, museum holdings, and folk arts and traditions. His mission coincided in time with one entrusted to Titus Burckhardt for the preservation of the old city of Fez, which explains why Michon has been invited by the Temenos Academy to share with the public both his personal memories and some documentation as a tribute to Burckhardt's unique personality and long and close relationship with Morocco.

Since retiring from the UN civil service in 1980, Dr. Michon has continued translating, including a French version of Martin Lings' book *Muhammad: His Life Based on the Earliest Sources*, and a French rendering of the Koran (see www.altafsir.com).

He continues to consult on projects related to the preservation of Islamic cultural heritage. Dr. Michon regularly participates in international conferences and symposia, and has, over the years, given many lectures on subjects connected to the value of art as a means of communication between people who belong to different cultures, as well as on the necessity of protecting traditional arts and crafts everywhere in the world.

In addition to all these studies and activities, Dr. Michon has continued to work out in the field: in Morocco, on a UNESCO project for the creation of a school of traditional arts and crafts in Fez, on the preparation and publication of the *Directory of Moroccan Handicrafts*, on the creation of CERKAS (Center for the Rehabilitation of Southern Kasbas) in Ouarzazate, and on proposals for the rehabilitation of Ksar Aït Ben Haddou (entered on the List of World Heritage in 1986); in Oman, on the restoration of the citadel of Bahla; in Bahrain, on the inventory of historical sites; and in Uzbekistan, on the evaluation of the state of conservation of historical sites in Itchan Kala, Bukhara, Samarkand, and Shahrisabz.

ROGER GAETANI is an editor, educator, and student of world religions who lives in Bloomington, Indiana. He has co-edited, with Jean-Louis Michon, the World Wisdom anthology on Islamic mysticism, *Sufism: Love and Wisdom*. He directed and produced the DVD compilation of highlights to the 2006 conference on Traditionalism entitled, *Tradition in the Modern World: Sacred Web 2006 Conference*, and has most recently edited the book, *A Spirit of Tolerance: The Inspiring Life of Tierno Bokar*.

Titles on Islam by World Wisdom

Art of Islam: Illustrated, by Titus Burckhardt, 2009

Christianity/Islam: Perspectives on Esoteric Ecumenism,
by Frithjof Schuon, 2008

Introduction to Sufi Doctrine, by Titus Burckhardt, 2008

Introduction to Traditional Islam, Illustrated: Foundations, Art, and Spirituality,
by Jean-Louis Michon, 2008

Islam, Fundamentalism, and the Betrayal of Tradition: Essays by Western Muslim Scholars,
edited by Joseph E.B Lumbard, 2004

The Mystics of Islam, by Reynold A. Nicholson, 2002

The Path of Muhammad: A Book on Islamic Morals and Ethics by Imam Birgivi,
interpreted by Shaykh Tosun Bayrak, 2005

Paths to the Heart: Sufism and the Christian East,
edited by James S. Cutsinger, 2003

Paths to Transcendence: According to Shankara, Ibn Arabi, and Meister Eckhart,
by Reza Shah-Kazemi, 2006

The Spirit of Muhammad: From Hadith,
edited by Judith and Michael Oren Fitzgerald, 2009

A Spirit of Tolerance: The Inspiring Life of Tierno Bokar,
by Amadou Hampaté Bâ, 2008

The Sufi Doctrine of Rumi: Illustrated Edition,
by William C. Chittick, 2005

Sufism: Love and Wisdom,
edited by Jean-Louis Michon and Roger Gaetani, 2006

Sufism: Veil and Quintessence, by Frithjof Schuon, 2007

Understanding Islam, by Frithjof Schuon, 1998

Universal Spirit of Islam: From the Koran and Hadith,
edited by Judith and Michael Oren Fitzgerald, 2006